Confessions of a Textbook Writer

If you promise not to get too mad, I'll tell you a secret. I used to write textbooks.

Yes, it's true. I helped write those big books that break your back when you carry them and put you to sleep when you read them. But let me say one thing in my own defense: I never meant for them to be boring!

I used to spend long days in the library, searching for stories to make my history textbooks fun to read. And I filled up notebooks with good ones—funny, amazing, inspiring, surprising, and disgusting stories. But as you've probably noticed, textbooks are filled with charts, tables, lists, names, dates, review questions . . . there isn't any room left for the good stuff. In fact, every time I tried to sneak in a cool story, my bosses used to drag me to this dark room in the basement of our building and take turns dropping filing cabinets on my head.

Okay, that's a lie. But they could have fired me, right? And I've got a wife and baby to think about.

So here's what I did: Over the years, I secretly stashed away all the stuff I wasn't allowed to use in textbooks. I kept telling myself, "One of these days I'm going to write my own history books! And I'll pack them with all the true stories and real quotes that textbooks never tell you!"

Well, now those books finally exist. If you can find it in your heart to forgive my previous crimes, I hope you'll give this book a chance. Thanks for hearing me out.

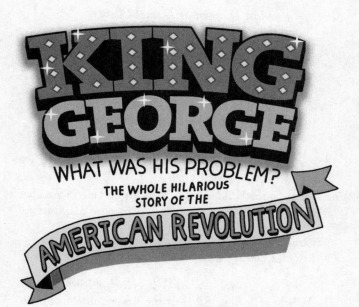

By Steve Sheinkin

*Most Dangerous: Daniel Ellsberg
and the Secret History of the Vietnam War*

*The Port Chicago 50:
Disaster, Mutiny, and the Fight for Civil Rights*

*Bomb: The Race to Build—and Steal—
the World's Most Dangerous Weapon*

*The Notorious Benedict Arnold:
A True Story of Adventure, Heroism & Treachery*

*Which Way to the Wild West?: Everything Your Schoolbooks
Didn't Tell You About America's Westward Expansion*

*Two Miserable Presidents: The Amazing, Terrible,
and Totally True Story of the Civil War*

*King George: What Was His Problem?
The Whole Hilarious Story of the American Revolution*

KING GEORGE

WHAT WAS HIS PROBLEM?
THE WHOLE HILARIOUS STORY OF THE
AMERICAN REVOLUTION

STEVE SHEINKIN

SQUARE
FISH

ROARING BROOK PRESS
New York

SQUARE
FISH

An Imprint of Macmillan Publishing Group, LLC
120 Broadway,
New York, NY 10271
mackids.com

Library of Congress Cataloging-in-Publication Data
Sheinkin, Steve.
King George : what was his problem? / Steve Sheinkin.
p. cm.
First published: The American Revolution / written and illustrated by Steve Sheinkin.
Stamford, CT : Summer Street Press, c2005, in series: Storyteller's history.
Includes bibliographical references and index.
ISBN 978-1-250-07577-2 (paperback)
1. United States—History—Revolution, 1775–1783—Juvenile literature. 2. United States—
History—Revolution, 1775–1783—Anecdotes—Juvenile literature.
I. Sheinkin, Steve. American Revolution. II. Title.
E208.S49 2008   973.3—dc22   2007039999

Published in the United States by Roaring Brook Press
This Square Fish Edition: 2015
Book designed by YAY! Design
Square Fish logo designed by Filomena Tuosto

20 19 18 17 16 15

AR: 6.4 / LEXILE: 880L

For Adriano, Louis, and all the other students
who showed me the light.
—S.S.

Contents

How to Start a Revolution

Entire books have been written about the causes of the American Revolution. You'll be glad to know this isn't one of them. But you really should understand how the whole thing got started. After all, if you ever find yourself ruled by someone like King George, you'll want to know what to do. So here's a quick step-by-step guide to starting a revolution.

Step 1: Kick Out the French

Let's pick up the action in 1750. Britain, France, and Spain had carved up North America into massive empires, as you can see on the map below. You'd think they'd be satisfied, right? But Britain and France both wanted to see their names on even more of the map. Let's face it, they both wanted the *whole* map. (It didn't bother them that most of the land actually belonged to Native Americans.)

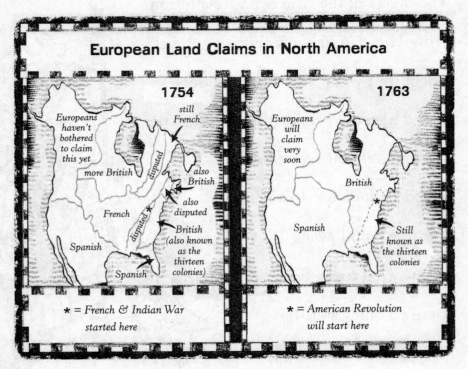

European Land Claims in North America

1754

Europeans haven't bothered to claim this yet

still French

more British

disputed

also British

also disputed

French

British (also known as the thirteen colonies)

disputed

Spanish

Spanish

★ = French & Indian War started here

1763

Europeans will claim very soon

British

Spanish

Still known as the thirteen colonies

★ = American Revolution will start here

To Britain and France, this seemed like a good reason to fight a war. You can call it the French and Indian War or the Seven Years War— either way, the British won. Britain took over most of France's land in North America. For Britain, this was the good news.

2

Step 2: Tax the Colonists

Here's the bad news: war is really expensive. The British were left with a mountain of debt. And now they had to keep 10,000 soldiers in North America to protect all their new land. That's not cheap. The British prime minister George Grenville started thinking of ways to raise some quick cash. You can guess the idea he came up with, can't you?

That's right: he decided to tax the British colonists. Grenville really felt that the thirteen colonies owed Britain the money. As he put it:

"The nation has run itself into an immense debt to give them protection; and now they are called upon to contribute a small share toward the public expense."

Grenville's plan was called the Stamp Act. When colonists signed any legal document, or bought paper goods like newspapers, books, or even playing cards, they would have to buy stamps too (the stamps showed that you had paid the tax). A few members of Parliament warned that the Stamp Act might spark protests in the colonies. But young King George III (he was twenty-two) liked the idea. He didn't expect any problems.

George Grenville

Step 3: Hang the Taxman

King George never did understand Americans. No one likes a tax increase, no matter what the reasons. Besides, the thirteen colonies had been pretty much governing themselves for years. And self-government obviously includes coming up with your own taxes. So colonists started shouting a slogan:

"No taxation

without representation."

Meaning basically, "We're not paying!"

Shouting is easy, but how do you actually avoid paying the tax? Samuel Adams of Boston had that fig-ured out. Adams was in his early forties, and he hadn't really found anything he was good at yet. His father once gave him one thousand pounds (a lot of money) to start a business. Samuel loaned half of it to a friend, who never paid him back. It's safe to say Samuel had no talent for business. All he wanted to do was write about politics and argue in town meetings. How far can that get you in life?

Tax Protester

Pretty far, actually. Because when the time came to protest the Stamp Act, Adams was ready to take the lead. He figured it like this: *The Stamp Act is supposed to go into effect in November 1765, right? Well, what if there's no one around to distribute the stamps? Then we won't have to buy them. Simple.*

The job of distributing the stamps in Boston belonged to a man

named Andrew Oliver. When Oliver woke up one morning in August, he was informed that a full-size Andrew Oliver doll was hanging from an elm tree in town. Pinned to the doll was a nice poem:

"What greater joy did New England see,

Than a stamp man hanging on a tree?"

It got worse. That night a crowd of Bostonians, yelling about taxes, cut down the doll and carried it to Oliver's house. They chopped off its head and set it on fire. Then they started breaking Oliver's windows.

As you can imagine, Andrew Oliver found this whole experience fairly frightening. He wasn't so eager to start giving out the stamps in Boston.

That was exactly how Adams had planned it. Similar scenes took place all over the thirteen colonies. Calling themselves Sons of Liberty, protesters gave plenty of stamp agents the Andrew Oliver treatment. The agents quit as fast as they could. (Can you blame them?) So when the tax went into effect, there was no one around to collect it.

Step 4: Try, Try Again

Back in London, the British government was forced to face a painful fact—there was no money in this Stamp Act deal. Parliament voted to repeal (get rid of) the tax. King George reluctantly approved this decision.

Colonists celebrated the news with feasts and dances. Boston's richest merchant, a guy named John Hancock, gave out free wine and put on a fireworks show outside his house. The happy people of New York City built a statue of King George and put it in a city park. (Remember that statue; it will be back in the story later.)

What the colonists didn't realize was that British leaders were already talking about new taxes. After all, the British government still needed money. And most leaders still insisted that Britain had every right to tax the Americans. King George was especially firm on this point. He was a very stubborn fellow.

So Parliament passed the Townshend Acts in 1767. When colonial merchants imported stuff like paint, paper, glass, and tea, they would now have to pay a tax based on the value of each item. Or would they?

Step 5: Refuse to Pay

Rather than pay the new taxes, colonists started boycotting (refusing to buy) British imports. Women were the driving force behind these boycotts. Hannah Griffitts of Pennsylvania expressed the determination of many colonial women in a poem:

"Stand firmly resolved and bid Grenville to see

That rather than Freedom, we'll part with our tea.

And well as we love the dear draught* when a'dry

As American Patriots our taste we deny."

John Hancock found another way to get around paying taxes. Hancock simply snuck his goods past the tax collectors. He knew that smuggling was illegal, but he didn't feel too guilty about it. To Hancock, smuggling seemed like a fair response to an unfair law.

Of course the British wanted to stop smugglers like Hancock. But you have to remember, colonists really hated these taxes. So any British official who tried too hard to collect taxes was taking a serious risk. Think of poor John Malcolm, for example. This British official was stripped to the waist, smeared with hot tar, and covered with feathers from a pillow. Then he was pulled through Boston in a cart, just to

Hannah Griffitts

**pronounced like "draft"*

make the humiliation complete. What was the worst thing about getting tarred and feathered? Malcolm said the most painful part was trying to rip the tar off his burned body. He mailed a box of his tar and feathers, with bits of his skin still attached, to the British government in London. They sympathized. They sent him money.

Then, in the spring of 1768, Hancock's ship *Liberty* (full of smuggled wine from France) was seized by tax agents in Boston. Furious members of the Sons of Liberty gathered at the docks, where Sam Adams was heard shouting:

"If you are men, behave like men! Let us take up arms immediately and be free!"

The Sons spent the night throwing stones at the tax collectors' houses. They even dragged a tax agent's boat out of the water and lit it on fire in front of John Hancock's house. The terrified taxmen escaped to an island in Boston Harbor.

Samuel Adams

Step 6: Send in the Warships

King George did not appreciate this form of protest. The world's most powerful country can't have its government employees hiding on an island—it doesn't look good. It was time to get tough with the colonists. In the words of Frederick North, one of the king's favorite advisors: "America must fear you before she can love you."

Why not just repeal the Townshend taxes? "I hope we shall never think of it," snapped North, "till we see America prostrate [facedown] at our feet."

North was another guy who didn't understand Americans.

In October 1768, British warships sailed into Boston Harbor. Under the command of General Thomas Gage, one thousand British soldiers marched off the ships and paraded through town in their bright red coats, beating drums and dragging cannons.

That should solve everything, right?

Well, nothing too serious happened until March 1770. On March 2, a British soldier named Patrick Walker was looking for a little extra work in Boston (the soldiers were paid almost nothing). He stopped by a ropewalk—an outdoor workshop where ropes were made—and spoke with a rope maker named William Green.

Green: *Soldier, do you want work?*
Walker: *Yes.*
Green: *Well then, go clean my outhouse.*

Only Green didn't say "outhouse." He used a word I can't print here. Walker was quite offended. He got a group of soldiers together, and they attacked the rope makers with wooden clubs. The rope makers fought back with clubs of their own. It was an ugly scene.

The point of this story is simple: the British soldiers and the people of Boston just weren't getting along. And it's easy to see why. The soldiers were in town to enforce laws that made people furious, and people took their anger out on the soldiers. Did the soldiers deserve such hatred? Maybe not. Most were seventeen- and eighteen-year-old boys from poor families. This was the only job they could get, and they hated being in Boston just as much as the people hated having them.

On the night of March 5, 1770 (three days after the ropewalk fight), all the anger in Boston exploded into violence.

Step 7: Fire into a Crowd

It was a cold night. There was a foot of snow on the ground. Sons of Liberty walked the streets in groups, wooden clubs in hand. They watched the soldiers, and the soldiers watched them. Both sides were expecting something to happen.

But no one thought it would begin with an apprentice wig maker named Edward Garrick. At about 8:30, young Garrick passed a British officer in the street. Garrick pointed to the officer and shouted:

"There goes the fellow that won't pay my master for dressing his hair!"

Edward Garrick

That's a serious insult, Ed—accusing a gentleman of not paying his debts. A young British soldier named Hugh White stepped forward to defend his officer. Garrick and White exchanged a few curses. Then White cracked Garrick in the head with the butt of his musket. Garrick went down, scrambled up, and yelped for help.

A crowd gathered quickly. At first it was just a few of Garrick's friends. Then people started coming from all over town. A man named Crispus Attucks led a group of fellow sailors from the wharf to the scene of the action. Attucks was six feet, two inches tall, about forty-five years old. He had escaped from slavery twenty years before. Witnesses said he had a stick or club in his hand.

Hugh White called out to his fellow soldiers for backup. Eight soldiers pushed their way through the mob to White. About three hundred people surrounded the soldiers, cursing at them and pelting them with snowballs, chunks of ice, even oyster shells. The soldiers pointed their loaded guns. The crowd shoved closer and closer to the blades of the British bayonets, shouting:

"You dare not fire!"

"You can't kill us all!"

Then there was a shot. Then a lot of shots. Then smoke and shocked silence. The crowd backed away. Crispus Attucks lay in the snow, killed instantly by two bullets through the chest. Six other men had also been shot. Four of them later died.

At a town meeting the next morning, Samuel Adams charged British soldiers with firing into a crowd of harmless protesters. As we have seen, this was not exactly true. Samuel was a gifted storyteller. He called the soldiers "bloody murderers." He gave the incident a name that everyone would remember: "the Boston Massacre."

Step 8: Keep the Tea Tax

After the Massacre, General Gage pulled the British soldiers out of Boston. This helped calm things down.

Over in Britain, leaders saw that the Townshend Acts were much more trouble than they were worth. Parliament voted to repeal the taxes. Well, most of them. They left a tax on tea. This was done on very specific instructions from King George:

"I am clear that there must always be one tax to keep up the right, and as such I approve the tea duty."

Sure, the king knew this small tea tax would not bring in any real money. He just wanted everyone to know that Britain still had the power to tax the colonies. Told you he was stubborn.

Step 9: Throw a Tea Party

On the night of December 16, 1773, a Boston shoemaker named George Hewes went into a blacksmith's shop and smeared coal dust on his face. He was hoping it would look like the war paint of a Mohawk Indian. It didn't, but that was okay. The main idea was to be in disguise. Hewes went out into the dark street with an ax in his hand. Dozens of men, all badly disguised as Indians, were marching down

King George III

to the waterfront. Hewes joined the strange parade.

Three ships full of British tea were tied up at a wharf in Boston Harbor. The people of Boston had refused to let the ship owners unload the cargo. They had no intention of paying the tea tax. So the tea sat in the ships, neatly packed in chests. Not for long.

George Hewes and the other disguised Sons of Liberty rowed out to the British ships. Communicating with only grunts and silent signals, about fifty men boarded each ship. They dragged the chests of tea up to the deck, chopped them open with axes, and dumped the tea into Boston Harbor.

Hundreds of people came down to the wharf to watch. Hewes even saw a few spectators sneak onto the ships to snag some of the tea: "There were several attempts," he recalled, "made by some of the citizens of Boston . . . to carry off small quantities of it for their family use. . . . They would watch for their opportunity to snatch up a handful from the deck, where it became plentifully scattered, and put it into their pockets."

Hewes caught one man shoving loose tea leaves into the lining of his coat. Hewes yanked off the coat, and the guy ran away.

It took about three hours to dump all the tea. Then, just to make sure no one was hiding any tea, each of the "Mohawks" was asked to take off his shoes and shake them out into the water.

When George Hewes finally got home that night, he told his wife, Sally, all about the Boston Tea Party.

Step 10: Pay the Fiddler

A British naval commander named Admiral Montagu watched the Boston Tea Party from the window of his waterfront house. As the disguised Sons of Liberty marched away from the wharf, Montagu opened his window and exchanged shouts with one of the men:

> Montagu: *Well, boys, you have had a fine, pleasant evening for your Indian caper, haven't you? But mind, you have got to pay the fiddler yet!*
>
> Son of Liberty: *Just come out here, if you please, and we'll settle the bill in two minutes.*

Montagu shut his window. The men cheered and laughed.

Montagu was right, though—the people of Boston would have to "pay the fiddler." In other words, they would have to face the consequences of their actions.

One consequence was that King George threw an absolute fit. He called the Tea Party "violent and outrageous." And he wasn't alone. Even members of Parliament who usually supported the Americans were furious about the destruction of British tea. A member of Parliament named Charles Van captured the angry mood in London, declaring:

"The town of Boston ought to be boxed about their ears and destroyed. I am of the opinion you will never meet with that proper obedience to the laws of this country until you have destroyed that nest of locusts."

Charles Van

Now, that's the kind of advice King George liked.

At the king's request, Parliament passed a series of laws designed to teach the people of Boston, once and for all, that British authority must be obeyed. No fooling around now. Parliament ordered the port of Boston shut down until the town paid for the ruined tea. The people of Massachusetts would no longer be allowed to elect their own judges or sheriffs. And if the residents of Boston wanted to hold a town meeting, they would need permission from British officials.

To enforce all this, General Thomas Gage was sent back to Boston—this time with four thousand British soldiers.

That should solve everything, right?

Step 11: Stand Firm

A few months later, Samuel Adams was eating dinner with his wife and kids when one of Boston's best tailors knocked on the door. The tailor came in and began measuring Sam's rather round body. He said he had been asked to make Adams a new suit. He refused to say who had paid for this service. Then a hatter arrived. He measured Adams's head for a new hat. He wouldn't say who had sent him. Then a shoemaker came to measure Adams's feet. What was going on?

Well, a lot. As planned, the British soldiers had closed the port of Boston. This was a kick in the gut to the Boston economy, which was built on shipping and trade. Stores shut, jobs disappeared. Colonists called the harsh British punishments the "Intolerable Acts." Even people who avoided politics took sides in the crisis: you were a Patriot if you opposed British taxes and stood by Boston; you were a Loyalist if you supported the king.

Patriots all over the colonies sent supplies to Boston: beef, fish, flour, rice, cash. Patriot leaders also agreed to hold a meeting in Philadelphia. They could all get to know each other, maybe figure out what to do about the Intolerable Acts.

That explains the tailor, hatter, and shoemaker. Of course, Sam Adams would be making the trip to Philadelphia for the Continental Congress. But for such an important meeting, he really needed some new clothes (he was an embarrassingly sloppy dresser). So his friends hired the tailor and the others. And Sam Adams set off for Congress in a fancy new suit with gold buttons on the sleeves (and silver buckles on his shoes). Next to him in the carriage sat his cousin John Adams, well-known lawyer, Patriot, and grump.

A few hundred miles south in Virginia, George Washington was also getting ready for the Congress. Washington was one of the few Patriot leaders with military experience (in the French and Indian War). He had recently made news with a bold promise:

"If need be, I will raise one thousand men, subsist them at my own expense, and march myself at their head for the relief of Boston."*

George Washington

*supply

Patrick Henry and Edmund Pendleton (two more Virginia Patriots) stopped by Washington's place, and they all set out together for Philadelphia.

As they rode off, a voice called out to them: "I hope you will all stand firm—I know George will."

That was Martha Washington, George's wife. And while she urged courage, she also worried where this conflict might lead, saying, "I foresee consequences. Dark days and darker nights."

Step 12: Make Speeches

The Continental Congress began in Philadelphia in early September 1774. There were a total of fifty-six delegates from twelve colonies (Georgia stayed home). Fifty-six men meant fifty-six different opinions—and some very long debates. John Adams complained that if someone had declared that three plus two equaled five, members would have wasted a couple of days debating the issue.

So it took a while, but the members of Congress came to some serious decisions. They declared the Intolerable Acts to be an illegal violation of the rights of American colonists. They decided it was time to start boycotting trade with Britain again. And they agreed that the colonies should start arming and training their militias (volunteer armies) just in case there was trouble with the British soldiers in Boston.

Before the Congress ended, Patrick Henry did two things that he was famous for. One, he annoyed everyone by talking too much. And two, he made a few fabulous speeches. "The distinctions between Virginians, Pennsylvanians, New Yorkers and New Englanders are no more," he cried. "I am not a Virginian, but an American."

This kind of unity really surprised British leaders. They had been sure that the other colonies would stand aside and let Massachusetts suffer alone.

Step 13: Let Blows Decide

Now the stage was set for a showdown. Neither side really wanted war, but neither side was willing to back down. As usual, King George thought a show of force would improve matters. He declared: "The New England colonies are in a state of rebellion. . . . Blows must decide whether they are to be subject to this country or independent."

Blows, you say? Speaking in a church in Virginia, Patrick Henry did his thing:

"Gentlemen may cry, 'Peace! Peace!' but there is no peace. . . .

I know not what course others may take, but as for me, give

me liberty or give me death!"

Back in Boston, all this tough talk was making General Gage extremely nervous. Unlike Patrick Henry and King George, Gage was going to have to do the actual fighting. He wrote to London, asking for more soldiers.

"If you think ten thousand men sufficient, send twenty," Gage wrote. And this takes us up to April 1775. Right where we want to be.

Patrick Henry

A Sleepless Night Before Revolution

What are you waiting for, Thomas Gage? That was basically the message from London. King George wanted action! He wanted General Gage to march his soldiers out of Boston and seize the military supplies that were being stored by local militias. He wanted Patriot troublemakers like Samuel Adams and John Hancock arrested and shipped to London in chains.

Orders Are Orders

Tensions in Boston were at record levels in the spring of 1775. General Gage was so worried about another Boston Massacre–type incident, he refused to allow his soldiers to carry their pistols in the street. For this sound judgment, the soldiers called Gage "the Old Woman."

Meanwhile, in the towns around Boston, thousands of militia members were just waiting for the British soldiers to make a move. Some militias even called themselves "minutemen," because they could be called together at a minute's notice (or pretty quickly, anyway).

Gage was sitting on a time bomb—and everyone could hear the ticking.

But orders are orders. The general considered his options. He knew that the local militias were storing their weapons in Concord, a town just seventeen miles northwest of Boston. And he knew that Samuel Adams and John Hancock were lying low at a house in Lexington. *Interesting.* . . .

So Gage came up with a plan. He'd send seven hundred British soldiers out to Lexington and Concord. They could try to grab Adams and Hancock in Lexington. Then they could march on to Concord and destroy the military supplies there. That should make the king happy, right?

Don't Open That Envelope

During the afternoon of April 18, 1775, Gage sat down at his desk and wrote out orders for the mission. He sealed the plan in an envelope without showing it to anyone. He gave the envelope to Colonel Francis Smith, who was to lead the expedition. He told Smith to have his soldiers assemble on Boston Common, by the Charles River, at exactly ten o'clock that night. He ordered Smith not to open the envelope with the plan until then.

Why would Gage keep the plan secret from the man who was going to lead the mission? Gage knew that it was going to be very dangerous for his soldiers to march out into the hostile territory around Boston. His hope was to keep the march secret until the very last second. Then his soldiers just might be able to get out to Concord and back before the minutemen had time to react.

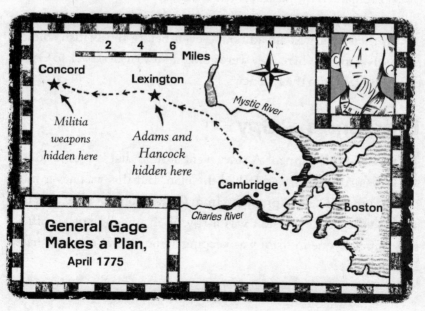

General Gage Makes a Plan, April 1775

Would Gage be able to keep the plan a secret? Listen to this: At about nine o'clock that night, Gage called his pal General Hugh Percy into his office and told him the plan. He told Percy that no one else knew of the plan yet.

Minutes later, Percy left Gage's house and walked out into Boston Common. He saw that British soldiers were quietly gathering down by the water, as planned. And he saw small groups of people, nosy Bostonians, standing around, watching the action. He snuck up to one group. His face hidden by shadows, Percy joined the conversation:

Bostonian: *The British troops have marched, but will miss their aim.*
Percy: *What aim?*
Bostonian: *Why, the cannon at Concord.*

So the secret was already out—even before the British soldiers themselves knew where they were going! Percy rushed back to Gage's office and told him the bad news.

Everyone's a Spy

How did this happen? A story went around that Gage's wife (she was American) had leaked the plan. But this was never more than a rumor. The real problem, from Gage's point of view, was that almost everyone in Boston was a spy. Well, maybe not an official spy, but everyone in town was keeping an angry eye on those hated British soldiers.

One of the men who organized this American spy ring was a silversmith named Paul Revere.

"I was one of upwards of thirty
who formed ourselves into
a committee for the purpose of
watching the movements of the
British soldiers."

People outside the city were also on the lookout. When General Gage first started thinking about sending his soldiers out to Concord, he realized that he would need to know more about the roads the army would have to take. He gave Colonel Francis Smith the job of secretly checking out the route. Smith took along a young private named John Howe.

Paul Revere

Smith and Howe dressed up like American laborers (you know: gray overcoat, leather pants, blue stockings). They grabbed a couple of walking sticks and set off on the seventeen-mile hike to Concord. Smith didn't make it too far before getting hungry (he was a famously big eater). So the two men went into a roadside tavern, sat at a table, and ordered some breakfast.

Pretending to be a regular old American in search of a job, Smith asked the waitress if she knew of any place where he and his friend might find some employment. But the woman (all we know about her is that she was African American) had spent a lot of time in Boston, and she knew the faces of the high-ranking British officers. She looked him in the eye and said:

"Smith, you will find employment enough for you and all Gage's men in a few months."

Smith just about fell off his chair. He called the woman a "saucy wench" and promised to kill her if he ever saw her again. Then he ran home.

"The last I saw of Smith he was running through barberry bushes to keep out of sight of the road," said Private Howe.

You get the idea—the British couldn't make a move without everyone knowing about it. And by April 18, it was really, really obvious that something was going on in Boston. British officers were stopping by the stables, making sure their horses were ready to go. Totally ignoring the lowly local kids who worked as stable boys, the officers bragged about the upcoming action. The stable boys passed the information on to Paul Revere.

Another clue: the British repaired their small transport boats and launched them in the Charles River. These were the boats the British soldiers would use if they ever wanted to cross the river on their way to Lexington and Concord. As Revere noted, "From these movements we expected something serious was to be transacted."

Trapped in Boston

So Revere and his fellow spies knew the British were about to do "something serious." But what?

It really wasn't that hard to guess. Everyone knew about the weapons in Concord, and everyone knew that King George wanted them destroyed. Everyone also knew that the king wanted John Hancock and Samuel Adams arrested. British soldiers made no secret of their hostile feelings for Hancock and Adams. One popular British marching chant went like this (you can sing along to the tune of "Yankee Doodle"):

"As for their King, John Hancock,

and Adams if they're taken,

their heads for signs shall hang on high,

upon that hill called Beacon."

It doesn't exactly rhyme, but you get the point: Hancock and Adams were wanted men. Any time your head is hanging up as a sign, it's not good.

On the night of April 18, British soldiers were gathering by the river. Revere and friends knew what they had to do. First: warn Hancock and Adams that British soldiers were on their way to arrest them. Second: alert the people of Concord that the British were coming to destroy the weapons stored there.

Easier said than done. Boston was nearly surrounded by water, so to get out of the city they had to either cross the Charles River or make it over the thin strip of land called Boston Neck. And of course,

Gage knew that Revere and other express riders would try to get a warning out to Lexington and Concord. Gage issued strict orders to his men: let no one out of Boston tonight! He moved the warship *Somerset* into the river to block any exit by boat. He placed a string of soldiers across Boston Neck (it was only sixty yards wide). He even sent out groups of British officers on horseback, pistols hidden under their coats, to patrol the road to Lexington and Concord.

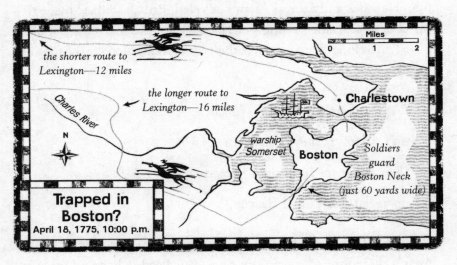

the shorter route to Lexington—12 miles

the longer route to Lexington—16 miles

Charles River

N

Miles
0 1 2

Charlestown

warship Somerset

Boston

Soldiers guard Boston Neck (just 60 yards wide)

Trapped in Boston?
April 18, 1775, 10:00 p.m.

"Two if by Sea"

There was a real chance that no one would be able to get out of Boston with a warning for the nearby towns. But don't worry: Revere and friends had a back-up plan. They arranged to send a secret signal by lighting lanterns at the top of Old North Church in Boston. The lanterns would be visible across the Charles River in Charlestown. This way, if no one could get out of Boston with the latest news, at least people in Charlestown could begin spreading the alarm that the British were on their way.

It was agreed that one lantern would mean the British were

marching out by land, over Boston Neck. Two lanterns would mean the British were coming by water, over the Charles River. Yes, these are the "One if by land, and two if by sea" lanterns from the famous Henry Wadsworth Longfellow poem.

The guy who volunteered to hang the lanterns was a young sexton at Old North Church, Robert Newman. A sexton cleans up the place, rings the church bells, stuff like that. Newman didn't like the job, but he kept it, he said, "because times are so hard."

Now it was just before ten o'clock, and Newman was ready for action. The first thing he did was say good night to his mom. And not just because he was a good son. British officers were renting rooms in the family house, and at this moment they were sitting around play-ing cards in the living room. Newman wanted the officers to think he was going to bed for the evening. In fact, he went up to his room, climbed out the window, climbed over the roof, and jumped down into the dark shadows in front of the church.

Revere found Newman there at a little after ten o'clock. Maybe Revere held up two fingers to silently show Newman that the British were moving out by water—this was clear by now, since the British soldiers were already gathering by the river. Newman knew what to do. He used his keys to unlock the church doors. He took two lanterns from the closet, climbed the stairs to the top of the bell tower, and lit the lanterns—but only for a moment. He didn't want the signal to be spotted by anyone on the warship *Somerset*, which was clearly visible in the water below.

Then Newman went down the stairs, put the lanterns back, leapt out a window in the back of the church, climbed up and over the roof of his mother's house, dropped in through the window of his bed-room, and lay down in bed.

You think he slept that night?

Across the River

As soon as Paul Revere left Robert Newman at the church door, he ran home to get his riding boots. Revere's mission was to row across the Charles River, if possible, and then ride out to Lexington with the warning. By now the streets were filled with British soldiers, armed for battle, marching toward their meeting point at the river. Avoiding the soldiers, Revere hustled from his house down to a spot on the water where he had a small rowboat hidden.

Two friends were waiting for Revere by the boat. They had agreed to row him across the river. But now that Revere and his friends looked out at the Charles, they realized that they had a problem. The *Somerset,* with its sixty-four guns, was sitting out there, keeping watch on the water. And just Revere's luck, it was a clear night with a big, bright moon. To have a chance, they would have to be absolutely silent.

Have you ever been in a rowboat? They make a lot of noise. The oars are held in place by metal oarlocks, which clank and squeak as the oars are pulled. To muffle this sound, Revere would need some cloth to wrap around the oarlocks. No one had thought of this ahead of time.

Luckily, one of Revere's friends had a girlfriend who lived on a nearby street. They rushed to her house. The guy gave a whistle outside his girl's window. She came to the window. He whispered for her to throw down some cloth. She quickly slipped off her flannel petticoat (a kind of slip worn under a dress) and tossed it down. Revere and his friends ripped up the petticoat, wrapped it around the oarlocks, and rowed right across the river without being heard or seen by sailors on the *Somerset.*

Revere and That Other Guy

A few pals were waiting for Revere on the Charlestown shore. They told him they had seen the lanterns just fine and had already started spreading the news. They warned him that British officers were out patrolling the roads. Then they gave him a fast horse and watched him set off on the most famous horseback ride in American history. "It was then about eleven o'clock," Revere remembered.

We know that Revere's first goal was to get to Lexington to warn Adams and Hancock. On the way there he warned people in houses along the road. Most people think that Revere shouted: "The British are coming! The British are coming!"

But what he probably said was:

"The regulars are out! The regulars are out!"

By "regulars" he meant British soldiers. He really should have said "The British are coming!" It sounds better. Oh, well—too late now.

Paul Revere gets all the press, but meanwhile a second express rider was also out that night. He was a twenty-three-year-old shoemaker named Billy Dawes. (This was another part of Revere's backup plan—if he got caught, maybe Dawes would get through with the warning.)

Paul Revere

To get out of Boston, Dawes first had to find a way past the British soldiers guarding Boston Neck. He was the perfect man for this risky job. He was the kind of guy who liked to sneak in and out of Boston pretending to be a drunken farmer, just for laughs. So he made it out on the night of April 18. Like Revere, he set out for Lexington. We'll catch up with him in a minute.

The Midnight Intruder

N ow let's check in on Samuel Adams and John Hancock, two guys who have done so much to cause all this trouble. Adams and Hancock were staying at the home of Reverend Jonas Clarke in Lexington. It was a full house at the Clarkes' place. In addition to Adams, Hancock, and the Clarke family (fourteen of them!), you also had Hancock's Aunt Lydia, his fiancée, Dorothy Quincy, and his clerk, John Lowell.

It was just after midnight, and everyone had gone to bed. The big house was dark and quiet. A Lexington minuteman named William Munroe stood guard outside the house, just in case.

Suddenly, a horse charged up and a man jumped off. He demanded to be let into the Clarkes' home. But Munroe didn't know this excited rider, and he asked him to keep his voice down. "I told him the family had just retired, and had requested that they might not be disturbed by any noise about the house," Munroe later said.

"Noise!" shouted the stranger. "You'll have noise enough before long. The regulars are coming out!"

The man pushed past Munroe and started pounding on the front door. Several windows opened upstairs, and several heads stuck out to investigate the disturbance. One of the heads (in a silk nightcap) belonged to John Hancock. He looked down at the door, recognized the intruder, and said:

"Come in, Revere, we are not

afraid of you."

Paul Revere was let in, and everyone came downstairs to hear the news.

John Hancock

Hancock immediately began pacing in his nightshirt, demanding his sword and gun, insisting that he was going out into Lexington Common to fight the British. He was probably trying to impress Dorothy. Samuel Adams, however, preferred to get out of town. He reminded Hancock that the two of them were members of the Continental Congress—politicians, in others words, not soldiers. That was his polite way of telling Hancock that he was acting like a fool. But Hancock continued to insist that he would stand and fight.

While Adams and Hancock are arguing this point, we'll check the progress of the British soldiers. Where were they, anyway? According to Gage's plan, they should have been here by now.

Where Are the British?

G age's whole plan was based on timing. He wanted his soldiers to hit Concord before dawn, before the minutemen had a chance to gather in large numbers. Gage's first mistake was putting Colonel Francis Smith in command of the expedition. Smith was a slow-moving man, one of those people who's always late. You'll remember that Gage ordered Smith to have his soldiers assembled by the boats at exactly ten o'clock. Well, the men were there, but Smith wasn't. When he finally showed up, about seven hundred soldiers were standing around, wondering what they were supposed to be doing.

From this point on, everything moved much too slowly. It took two trips to get all the soldiers across the Charles River. Once they were on the other side, the men stood around waiting some more. Lieutenant John Barker remembered: "We were halted in a dirty road and stood there till two o'clock in the morning, waiting for provisions to be brought from the boats and to be divided."

This was a total waste of time, since most of the men had brought their own food. As soon as they got their share of army food, they threw it on the ground.

So four hours were gone already, and the British had traveled about a quarter of a mile. Not a good start. At least they were on their way now, marching toward Lexington in the bright moonlight.

On to Concord

A nd speaking of Lexington, Billy Dawes arrived at the Clarkes' house while we were checking on the British. Don't blame him for getting there half an hour after Revere—his route was longer.

While Dawes and Revere had a quick snack (you have to eat, even in the middle of famous historical events), Captain John Parker got the Lexington minutemen together on the town common. They had their guns. They were ready to defend their town. The only problem was, there was nothing to do. The British were nowhere in sight.

It was a cold night. Parker couldn't keep his men standing out there forever. So he let the men go, but told them to listen for William Diamond beating his drum. This was the signal for the minutemen to come running back to Lexington Common. Some of the men went home. Others walked across the common to Buckman's Tavern, where they waited with a drink by the warm fire.

At about one a.m., Revere and Dawes left the Clarkes' house. Riding on very tired horses, they started down the road toward Concord. They still had to warn the people there that . . . well, you know what. On their way out of Lexington, they met up with Samuel Prescott, a young doctor from Concord. Prescott was heading home from his fiancée Lydia's house. He offered to help spread the alarm with Revere and Dawes. The three of them set off together.

Now, remember those armed British officers that General Gage sent out to patrol the roads? They're about to make a sudden appearance.

Captured!

On the way to Concord, Prescott and Dawes stopped to warn people in a house beside the road. Revere rode up ahead a bit, just to check out the path. He spotted two British officers hiding in the shadows of a tree. They spotted him too. Then a lot of things happened very quickly.

Revere shouted a warning to Prescott and Dawes. A few more British officers charged out from the shadows, pointing their pistols and shouting: "If you go an inch further, you are a dead man!" This didn't stop anyone. Revere, Prescott, and Dawes all dashed off in different directions.

Prescott jumped his horse over a stone wall and raced down the road. Dawes tried to trick the British by pretending to be one of them. "Haloo, boys, I've got two of 'em!" he yelled, galloping his horse toward the woods. But then, for some reason, he fell off. He scrambled to his feet and darted into the dark woods on foot. (Dawes's watch flew out of his pocket when he fell from his horse. A few days later, when the coast was clear, he came back and found it.)

Revere also raced his horse toward the woods. But he rode right to a spot where six more British officers were hiding. They stepped out of the shadows, held their guns on Revere, and started questioning him:

British Officer: *Sir, may I crave your name?*
Revere: *My name is Revere.*
British Officer: *What, Paul Revere?*
Revere: *Yes.*

These guys knew who Paul Revere was, and they had a good idea of what he had been doing. Revere never forgot what happened next: "One of them . . . clapped his pistol to my head, called me by name and told me he was going to ask me some questions, and if I did not give him true answers, he would blow my brains out."

Revere admitted that he had been out warning people that the British army was on its way. The British cursed at him and kept threatening to shoot him. But they had to patrol the road, and they didn't want to worry about keeping an eye on him. So they took his horse and let him go.

Revere stumbled through pastures and a graveyard on his way back to Lexington. Meanwhile, Dawes was somewhere in the woods, without a horse. If anyone was going to get to Concord in time to warn the town, it would have to be Prescott. Good thing he had stayed so late at Lydia's.

They Haven't Left Yet?

Revere made it back to the Reverend Clarke's house in Lexington at about 3:30 in the morning. And guess what? Adams and Hancock were still there! With the British soldiers marching closer and closer, Hancock would not stop insisting that he was going to stay and fight. Dorothy Quincy recalled:

"Mr. Hancock was all night cleaning his gun and sword, and was determined to go out to the plain by the meeting-house where the battle was, to fight with the men who had collected."

Dorothy Quincy

Finally, somehow, Adams convinced Hancock that they'd better get going. A carriage was prepared for their escape. Before Hancock climbed in, he had time for one last argument, this time with his fiancée. Dorothy mentioned that she was going to go back to her father's house in Boston. Hancock objected:

Mr. Hancock: *No, madam, you shall not return as long as there is a British bayonet left in Boston!*
Ms. Quincy: *Recollect, Mr. Hancock, I am not under your authority yet. I shall go to my father's house tomorrow!*

Poor Adams must have been rolling his eyes in the back of the carriage. At least the argument was short. In a minute, Adams and Hancock made their escape.

Dorothy wasn't sorry to see John's carriage drive away. "At that time, I should have been very glad to have got rid of him," she said.

She and Aunt Lydia stayed behind at the Clarkes' house. Later that morning, from the second-story window, they watched the American Revolution begin.

Beat That Drum, Billy

Now it was a few minutes after four a.m. You know that cold, gray light that comes just before sunrise? That's how it was in Lexington when the British army was finally spotted on the road outside town. They were a mile away, and coming on fast. Captain Parker told sixteen-year-old William Diamond to start beating his drum.

The Lexington minutemen grabbed their guns and ran into town.

Who Fired the Shot Heard 'Round the World?

As their wagon rattled out of Lexington on the morning of April 19, Samuel Adams and John Hancock could only guess at what was going on back in town. They heard William Diamond's drum beating, and they knew what that meant. A few minutes later they heard a gunshot. Then a huge burst of gun- fire.

A Glorious Morning?

When Samuel Adams heard the explosion of gunfire from Lexington, he had a pretty good idea of what had just happened.

"Oh, what a glorious morning is this," he said.

John Hancock thought Adams was talking about the weather, which was not bad, but not glorious. Adams clarified: "I mean, what a glorious morning *for America*."

What was so glorious about it? Adams must have been thinking that those early-morning shots would be the start of a long, hard fight for American independence.

Hancock must have been thinking about lunch. He sent a messenger back to Lexington, instructing Dorothy and Aunt Lydia to meet him in Woburn (where Adams and Hancock were now headed). He told them to "bring the fine salmon" that they had planned to eat that day.

Wait a minute. The American Revolution just started, and we're talking about salmon. What just happened back there on Lexington Common?

Gathering Evidence

We're not exactly sure. British and American witnesses tell different versions of the story. You'll have to listen to some of the evidence and come to your own conclusions.

Just after sunrise on April 19, 1775, Major John Pitcairn led the first group of British troops into Lexington. This guy was itching for a fight, as he had recently written:

"I am satisfied that one active campaign, a smart action, and burning two or three of their towns, will set everything to rights. Nothing now, I'm afraid, but this will ever convince those foolish bad people that England is in earnest."

John Pitcairn

Nice guy, huh? But Pitcairn wasn't supposed to stop in Lexington on April 19. He and his men were out in front of the other British soldiers because they were rushing on to Concord. Their mission: get to Concord as quickly as possible and take control of the bridges in town. Remember, the British were already hours behind schedule. So Pitcairn was hoping to march right through Lexington.

Then he saw the Lexington minutemen lined up on the town common. There were about seventy of them, ranging in age from sixteen to sixty-five. There were eight father-and-son combinations. There was at least one African American, a thirty-four-year-old man named Prince Estabrook.

John Parker

When Captain John Parker saw the British approaching, he told his nervous minutemen:

"Let the troops pass by and don't molest them without they begin first."

The minutemen really weren't there to fight, anyway. They mostly wanted to send the British a message: We're here, we have guns, we don't appreciate your visit.

Pitcairn and his soldiers marched right up to the minutemen. No one knew what was about to happen.

The First Shot

One interesting thing about this moment is that both commanders told their men not to fire. Pitcairn gave very clear orders to the British soldiers: "I instantly called to the soldiers not to fire but to surround and disarm them."

John Parker gave similar orders to the minutemen: "I immediately ordered our troops to disperse and not to fire."

So while the British tried to surround the minutemen, the minutemen started slowly walking off in different directions. It was a confusing scene. The key point was this: the minutemen did not drop their guns. This angered the excitable

Major Pitcairn, who started shouting, "You villains, you rebels! Lay down your arms! Why don't you lay down your arms?"

And now, in the middle of all this chaos, someone fired. Who? According to minuteman Sylvanus Wood: "There was not a gun fired by any of Captain Parker's company, within my knowledge. I was so situated that I must have known it."

But British lieutenant John Barker told a different story: "On our coming near them they fired one or two shots."

So no one takes credit for "the shot heard 'round the world"—the first shot of the American Revolution. It might have been a minute-man, or it might have been a British soldier. It might even have come from one of the houses in town. What we do know is that when the British soldiers heard the shot, they lost control. They started charging, screaming, and firing their guns. "Our men without any orders rushed in upon them, fired and put 'em to flight," said Lieutenant Barker. "The men were so wild, they could hear no orders."

Some of the minutemen stood and fired back. Others ran for their lives, blasting away as they retreated through town.

Three Cheers

The shooting on Lexington Common lasted about ten minutes. It finally ended when Colonel Francis Smith (he's in charge of this mission, remember?) rode into town. Smith found a British drummer and ordered him to beat the "cease fire" signal. This worked.

Eight minutemen had been killed and nine more were wounded (including Prince Estabrook, who was shot in the shoulder). The wounded men crawled to nearby houses for help. Only one British soldier had been shot and slightly hurt.

It took Smith about half an hour to get the seven hundred British boys calmed down and organized. He spent a little time yelling at the men for losing control. He warned them to follow orders next time. Then he let them give three cheers for their "victory," and they marched on to Concord.

Salmon Update

Dorothy Quincy and Aunt Lydia watched the whole thing from the window of the Clarkes' house. When the shooting started, Lydia leaned out the window to get a closer look. A bullet whistled past her head and crashed into the barn next door. She pulled her head in.

After the British left town, the two women set off in a carriage to meet up with Hancock and Adams. Yes, they remembered to bring Hancock's "fine salmon." The salmon was cooked at a house in Woburn, and everyone was sitting down to lunch when a man ran in and started shouting that the British were on their way. So the fish was left behind and Adams and Hancock rode farther from the fighting. Later that day, they ate some cold pork and potatoes.

"Grand Music"

Now the action shifted down the road to Concord, where the Concord minutemen were ready and waiting. How did they know the British were coming?

"This morning, between one and two o'clock, we were alarmed by the ringing of the bell," explained Reverend William Emerson of Concord.

Who brought you the warning, Reverend?

"The intelligence was brought to us first by Dr. Samuel Prescott," Emerson said.

Prescott was the one who had escaped from the British patrol the night before. He raced into Concord and started spreading the news.

By seven in the morning, about 250 Concord minutemen were gathered in town. They weren't sure what to do, though. They talked it over. They decided to march out to meet the British.

A Concord minuteman named Amos Barrett remembered parading out of town with the group, a few of the men proudly playing their drums and fifes (small flutes). Then, out on the narrow road, they saw the seven hundred British soldiers coming toward them. They stopped. They realized they hadn't really thought this plan through very well. They turned around and marched back into Concord, with the British right behind. Both armies had their drummers and fifers going strong. "We had grand music," said Amos Barrett.

Barrett and the minutemen marched up into the hills above the town and waited to see what the British were going to do. The Americans had time on their side. The alarm had been spreading from town to town all morning, and more minutemen were pouring in from the towns around Concord. Soon there were 300 minutemen in the hills. Then 350, then 400.

There were also lots of people from town, mostly kids who were up there to watch. It was getting crowded. The minutemen had to ask the spectators to go somewhere else.

Josiah Haynes was the oldest man to fight that day. This seventy-nine-year-old minuteman had gotten up at dawn, grabbed his musket, and marched eight miles to Concord. Now he was glaring down at the North Bridge, and at the British soldiers guarding the bridge. He told the captain of his town's militia:

"If you don't go and drive them British from that bridge, I

shall call you a coward."

Hold on there, Josiah. Everyone was still hoping this day would end without more bloodshed.

Breakfast Time

Josiah Haynes

Down in town, British soldiers started looking for weapons. That was the whole idea of this mission, as Gage's secret orders to Colonel Smith explained: "You will seize and destroy all the artillery, ammunition, provisions, tents, small arms and all military stores whatever. But you will take care that the soldiers do not plunder the inhabitants or hurt private property."

Unfortunately for Gage, the people of Concord had been expecting something like this for days. By now nearly all of the military supplies were hidden in attics or buried in fields.

At the Wood family home, for example, a pile of guns had been hastily shoved into a bedroom. When the British came to search this house, the Wood women welcomed the soldiers. They told the men they could search anywhere they wished—except for one small bedroom where a sick woman was sleeping. The British officers considered themselves gentlemen, and they would never disturb a sick woman. So they ordered their men to leave that room alone.

Needless to say, no weapons were found in the Wood house.

Meanwhile, Colonel Smith and some of the other British officers set up chairs on people's lawns and started ordering breakfast. These guys were used to being served. Women in Concord grumbled and gave a few lectures on the rights of Americans. But they were willing to make a little money. They sold the officers meals of meat, potatoes, and milk.

All the while, the soldiers kept up their search for supplies. They found a few barrels of flour and some musket balls. They tossed it all into a pond. (A few days later the people fished everything out. Most of the flour was still good.) They found a few cannons, and they destroyed them. They smashed up the wooden carriages that were used to haul the cannons around. Then they set the broken wood on fire. That fire changed a lot of lives.

Just ask Hannah Davis.

The Bridge Fight

Early that morning Hannah Davis had watched the Acton minutemen gather outside her house. (Acton was a town near Concord.) Her husband, Isaac, was their captain. She later said:

Hannah Davis

"My husband said but little that morning. As he led the company from the house, he turned himself round, and seemed to have something to communicate. He only said, 'Take good care of the children,' and was soon out of sight."

Now, up in the hills, Isaac Davis and the other minutemen saw smoke rising from the middle of Concord. They were too far away to see that the smoke was just from the burning cannon carriages.

"Will you let them burn the town down?" shouted one minuteman.

"No! No!" the other men roared.

Captain Davis led the minutemen down toward the North Bridge. "We were all ordered to load," said Amos Barrett, "and had strict orders not to fire till they fired first, then to fire as fast as we could."

At the North Bridge, a British officer named Walter Laurie looked up and saw four hundred angry Americans marching toward him. Laurie didn't have much time to form a plan. A few British soldiers ran onto the bridge and started trying to rip up the wooden planks. The Americans called out for the British to stop messing with their bridge. Then the shooting started. As usual, no one knows who fired first.

"We soon drove them from the bridge," reported Amos Barrett. Several minutemen and British soldiers were killed or wounded. Isaac Davis was one of the men who died at the North Bridge.

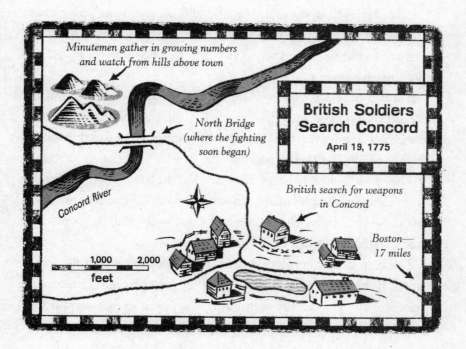

Minutemen gather in growing numbers and watch from hills above town

North Bridge (where the fighting soon began)

Concord River

British Soldiers Search Concord

April 19, 1775

British search for weapons in Concord

Boston— 17 miles

1,000   2,000
feet

This bridge fight is remembered as a major moment in American history. That's because up to this point, neither the minutemen nor the British soldiers had really expected the day's tense events to explode into all-out battle. Now men on both sides had been killed. Now it was going to be a long, bloody day. A long, bloody day that would lead to seven years of war.

The Nightmare Begins

And the British were not prepared for a long, bloody day. They hadn't even bothered to bring an army surgeon with them.

Colonel Smith stood in the middle of Concord, wondering what to do. Every time he lifted his telescope to the hills around town he saw more minutemen up there. He really had no choice. He had to make a run for Boston.

It was a little after noon when the British army marched out of Concord. No drums and fifes this time—the march was quick and quiet for about ten minutes. Were the minutemen hiding in the woods along the road? The British had no idea.

They found out when they hit a bend in the road called Meriam's Corner (home of Abigail and Nathan Meriam). Hundreds of minutemen opened fire from behind trees and stone walls. Bullets zoomed at the British from all sides.

The British soldiers started running, hoping to get past the minutemen. But the bullets kept coming. They kept coming for the next six hours. "We were totally surrounded with such an incessant fire as it's impossible to conceive," said Lieutenant Barker.

The minutemen had no organized plan. But there were a lot of them—about 3,600 men from more than forty different towns showed up before the day ended. They were able to line the road all the way to Boston. Men would shoot, duck back into the woods, reload their muskets, run forward, and shoot again. Minuteman (and Reverend) Edmund Foster explained the strategy like this: "Each sought his own place and opportunity to attack and annoy the enemy from behind trees, rocks, fences, and buildings."

The British soldiers must have felt like they had wandered into a nightmare. "We at first kept our order and returned their fire as hot as we received it," said a soldier named Henry de Berniere. But they were still fifteen miles from Boston! And soon they started running out of ammunition. The men panicked. "We began to run rather than retreat in order," de Berniere said.

Wounded men who could still walk held on to horses for support and hobbled along as fast as they could. Badly wounded and dead soldiers were left lying in the road.

Battling Brothers

I t was dark when the fighting finally ended. More than 250 British soldiers had been shot, and seventy-three of them died. About one hundred Americans had been hit, half of them killed. Seventy-nine-year-old Josiah Haynes was killed while reloading his musket.

That evening John Adams stood on a hill in Boston, watching the surviving British soldiers stumble back into town. It's hard for us to imagine what a shocking scene this must have been. Keep in mind that even Patriots like Adams still considered themselves citizens of the British Empire. "When I reflect and consider," wrote Adams, "that the fight was between those whose parents but a few generations ago were brothers, I shudder at the thought, and there's no knowing where our calamities will end."

What Next?

You won't be surprised to learn that British and American soldiers told very different versions of the amazing events of April 19, 1775.

According to General Thomas Gage, British soldiers had marched out to Concord on a simple, peaceful errand. Then, for no reason, they were viciously attacked by sneaky rebels! "A number of armed persons," he reported, "to the amount of many thousands, assembled on the 19th of April last, and from behind walls and lurking holes, attacked a detachment of King's Troops."

According to the Americans, a pack of bloodthirsty British soldiers had invaded the quiet towns of Lexington and Concord. Then, for no reason, the soldiers started shooting people. Express riders raced from town to town with letters saying: "The barbarous murders committed on our innocent brethren on Wednesday the 19th . . . have made it absolutely necessary that we immediately raise an army to defend our wives and children from the butchering hands of an inhuman soldiery."

Militiamen all over New England responded to the call by grabbing their guns and marching toward Boston. By the end of April, nearly 20,000 of them had gathered. They had the British army trapped in Boston. They had no idea what to do next.

King George knew what to do next. He was outraged that colonists had dared to fight with British soldiers. And he was more convinced than ever that the British military would soon bring the Americans to their knees. He said, "When once these rebels have felt a smart blow, they will submit."

Okay, George. We'll test your theory next.

George Washington, Meet Your Army

King George was hoping to smack the rebels with a "smart blow." But he was about to be disappointed. Before sunrise on the morning of May 10, 1775, a Vermont Patriot named Ethan Allen stepped into a boat on Lake Champlain. Allen and his men pushed out into the cold, choppy water and began silently rowing across the lake. The second blow of the American Revolution was about to be delivered.

And not by the British.

Here Comes Ethan Allen

This story begins in early May 1775, when a Connecticut lawyer named Noah Phelps stopped shaving. Once he had a nice little beard going, he disguised himself as a poor peddler—a guy who sells pots and tools door-to-door. Then he walked right up to the gates of Fort Ticonderoga, a British fort in northern New York.

The British soldiers asked the sloppy-looking peddler what he wanted. Phelps said he needed a shave. Could the fort's barber help him out? The soldiers let Phelps into the fort.

While Phelps sat still in the barber's chair, his eyes spied the condition of the fort. Crumbling walls, bored soldiers . . . it was just as he had hoped. Fort Ti (as the locals called it) was not prepared for an attack.

Noah Phelps passed the information on to the Green Mountain Boys, a group of Patriot farmers from the Green Mountains of Vermont. The Boys were led by Ethan Allen. Standing six foot six, with a furious temper, Allen was not the kind of guy you would want to have as an enemy. He was known to beat up two men at once by lifting them off the ground and banging them together.

But on the morning of May 10, Ethan Allen was perfectly calm. He and about eighty of the Boys rowed across Lake Champlain, reaching the New York side of the lake just before sunrise. There, in front of them, was their target: Fort Ticonderoga. One British soldier sat guarding the fort's gates. Or, he was supposed to be guarding the gates. Technically, he was asleep.

Party at Fort Ti

What woke the guard that morning? Probably it was the sound of eighty-three large Americans charging toward him, whooping and screaming like wild animals. The sleepy soldier stood up, lifted his gun, fired once, threw the gun on the ground, and ran into the fort, leaving the gates open behind him.

Ethan Allen and the Green Mountain Boys were right on his heels.

Inside the fort, a British officer named Jocelyn Feltham sat up suddenly in bed. "I was awakened by a number of shrieks," he explained. "I jumped up . . . I ran undressed to knock at Captain Delaplace's door."

Captain Delaplace was the commander of the fort. But he was still asleep. So Lieutenant Feltham went back to his room, grabbed some clothes, and stepped out into the hall.

And next thing he knew he was standing face to face with a very excited giant named Ethan Allen. Allen was knocking on Delaplace's door and shouting things like "Come out of there, you old rat!"

Lieutenant Feltham tried to appear calm and in control (which is hard to do when you have your pants in your hand). He demanded to know by what authority Ethan Allen was attacking this British fort. Allen roared back:

"In the name of the Great Jehovah

and the Continental Congress!"

Ethan Allen

This was a cool-sounding answer, and it later became famous. But at the time Lieutenant Feltham just seemed confused. "He began to speak again," Allen later wrote, "but I interrupted him and, with my drawn sword over his head, again demanded an immediate surrender."

The sword over the head did the trick—Feltham surrendered Fort Ticonderoga to the Americans. Within minutes, the Green Mountain Boys found ninety gallons of rum in the fort's cellar. The party lasted three days.

More important, Ethan Allen and the Boys had captured more than one hundred British cannons. If the Americans were really going to fight a war with Britain, they would need those big guns.

Walk with Me, Sam

B ut were the Americans going to fight a war with Britain? That question was still being debated down in Philadelphia.

One early morning in June, John and Samuel Adams met to talk over current events. "I walked with Mr. Samuel Adams in the State House yard," remembered John, "for a little exercise and fresh air, before the hour of Congress."

The Adams cousins knew that many members of the Continental Congress were not too thrilled about Ethan Allen's Fort Ti attack. These members were still hoping to find a peaceful solution to their conflict with the British government. In fact, Congress actually ordered Allen to make a careful list of all the items found at Fort Ticonderoga. That way they could give everything back to the British if war was avoided.

John and Samuel thought this was ridiculous. Wasn't it obvious by now that King George was never going to compromise? It was time for the thirteen colonies to join together, form one big army, and fight for independence.

In fact, John had decided that this was the day that he would try to convince Congress to pick a leader for the new American army. But who should that leader be? He wanted Samuel's advice. The cousins knew their friend John Hancock expected to be offered the job. And Hancock was definitely one of the most famous and popular Patriot leaders. The thing is, Hancock didn't know anything about leading an army. That could be a problem.

Besides, the cousins agreed, the American army should represent all regions of the colonies. The perfect thing would be to pick a leader from Virginia, the biggest of the southern colonies. That would help unite Americans in the long fight ahead. If only there was someone from Virginia, someone known and respected by everyone, someone with army experience, someone smart, tough, committed to the cause. . . .

John Adams Loses a Friend

"When Congress assembled, I rose in my place," said John Adams. It was time, Adams told Congress, to create a Continental army, with soldiers from all thirteen colonies. And it was time to elect a leader of the army. Members leaned forward in their seats. Who was Adams about to name?

John Hancock listened with a proud grin on his face. He really thought he was about to hear his name.

And John Adams enjoyed toying with Hancock a little bit. He made sure to keep an eye on Hancock's face as he named the man he believed should command the Continental army: "George Washington."

Hancock's smile collapsed in an instant. "I never remarked a more sudden and striking change of countenance [facial expression]," Adams said. Then Samuel Adams announced that he too supported Washington, which upset Hancock even more. "Mr. Hancock never loved me so well after this event as he had done before," John Adams remembered.

Meanwhile, George Washington jumped up and ran out of the room. He wanted to give everyone a chance to talk about him without worrying they might hurt his feelings.

So Washington waited outside while the other members of Congress decided whether or not he should lead the American Revolution.

George Washington, Love Poet

Was George Washington, age forty-three, about to be offered the opportunity of a lifetime? Or was he about to be handed an impossible job? Possibly both? He must have wondered about this as he waited in the library.

As a boy in Virginia, George had dreamed of becoming a military hero. He even tried to run away from home and join the British navy when he was fourteen. But his mother discovered the plan and refused to let him go. She was a very protective mom—and a bit stingy, too. Young George once asked her for money so he could take music lessons. She offered to *lend* him the cash.

So George never learned to play the violin. But he did spend some time working on his love poetry. Here's part of a letter he sent to Francis Alexander, a young woman he admired (notice that the first letters of each line spell out her name):

"From your bright sparkling eyes, I was undone;

Rays, you have more transparent than the sun,

Amidst its glory in the rising day,

None can you equal in your bright array . . ."

On June 16, 1775, George Washington sat down to write a very different letter. This time he was writing to his wife, Martha (or, as he called her in his letters, "my dear Patsy"). Congress had just made it official: George Washington was the commander of the new Continental army.

"I am now set down to write to you on a subject which fills me with inexpressible concern," wrote George to Martha. "It has been determined in Congress, that the whole army raised for the defense of the American cause shall be put under my care."

Why was Washington filled with concern? How would you feel if the future of an entire country were placed in your hands? Washington told Congress, "I this day declare, with utmost sincerity, I do not think myself equal to the command."

Young George

But there was no time for doubts or worries. Washington packed up his things and headed north to join the army, which was camped outside of Boston. While he was on his way, a messenger brought Washington some urgent news: a major battle had just been fought in Boston. When he heard the report, Washington said—Wait a second, let's check on the battle first. *Then* we'll hear what Washington said about it.

A Little Elbow Room

The last time we were in Boston was two months ago, just after the battles of Lexington and Concord. The British soldiers were trapped in town, surrounded by thousands of American militiamen.

That was still the situation in June 1775, when a new team of British generals arrived from London. One of the generals, John Burgoyne, was shocked to see a bunch of angry farmers holding the mighty British army in a trap.

"What! Ten thousand King's troops shut up? Well, let us get in, and we'll soon find elbow room."

John Burgoyne

So the British decided to get themselves a little elbow room. The first step was to seize control of Breed's Hill and Bunker Hill, two hills above Boston. From this high ground, they could start blasting away at the American camp.

But remember all those Patriot spies in and around Boston? They learned the British plans and got the news to the American soldiers. And the Americans beat the British to the hills.

Get Ready for a Long Day

Peter Brown was one of about twelve hundred Americans who spent the night of June 16 on Breed's Hill, building a fort of earth and logs. "We worked there undiscovered till about five in the morning," Brown later told his mother. After a tense and tiring night of work, the men were ready for bed. "Fatigued by our labor," he explained, "having no sleep the night before, very little to eat, no drink but rum . . . we grew faint, thirsty, hungry, and weary."

But there was no rest in sight. When the sun rose, the British looked up at Breed's Hill. They were used to seeing cows and sheep grazing up there. Now, all of a sudden, there was a fort! They quickly began blasting cannons up at Breed's Hill. "The enemy fired very warm from Boston and from on board their ships," Peter Brown reported.

Colonel William Prescott, the American commander on the hill, saw the rising fear in his men's eyes. Most of these guys had never been in a battle before. Prescott tried to keep them calm by walking up and down on the top of the fort's walls—he wanted to show them it was safe.

It wasn't safe.

A cannonball came bouncing into the fort and took off a man's head. "He was so near me," Prescott remembered, "that my clothes were besmeared with his blood and brains, which I wiped off, in some degree, with a handful of fresh earth."

None of the men had ever seen anything this awful before. It was about to get worse. The men looked down and saw more than two thousand British soldiers gathering below Breed's Hill.

The Battle of Bunker Hill

The British starting marching up the hill. Colonel Prescott knew his men had only about fifteen rounds of ammunition each. Knowing they would have to make every shot count, Prescott gave the guys some famous last-second advice:

"Don't fire till you see the whites of their eyes."

If you think the Americans had it bad, though, look at it from the British point of view. The British soldiers were now hiking uphill through thick grass, carrying 125 pounds of equipment under a blazing sun.

William Prescott

They were marching in nice, neat rows (making themselves easy targets) because the generals considered that the most "honorable" way to fight. And they were marching right up to the front of the American fort.

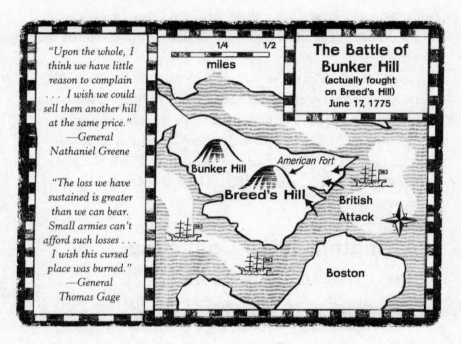

"Upon the whole, I think we have little reason to complain . . . I wish we could sell them another hill at the same price."
—General Nathaniel Greene

"The loss we have sustained is greater than we can bear. Small armies can't afford such losses . . . I wish this cursed place was burned."
—General Thomas Gage

1/4   1/2
miles

The Battle of Bunker Hill
(actually fought on Breed's Hill)
June 17, 1775

Bunker Hill

American Fort

Breed's Hill

British Attack

Boston

All over Boston, thousands of people stood watching from church steeples and the roofs of houses.

The British soldiers marched to within about one hundred feet of the fort, and they kept coming. Ninety feet, eighty feet, seventy . . . then the American guns exploded. The British were blown backwards. A British officer named Francis Rawdon said: "They rose up and poured in so heavy a fire upon us that the oldest officers say they never saw a sharper action."

The Americans cheered and waved their hats as the surviving British soldiers tripped down the hill.

The British officers told their men to turn around and attack again. They were driven back down the hill a second time. So the British charged up the hill a third time. And they finally captured the fort, though at an awful cost—one thousand British soldiers were shot that day.

Even though most of the fighting took place on Breed's Hill, this battle became known as the battle of Bunker Hill. No one seems to know why. The important thing is that the Americans were proud of the battle of Bunker Hill (though when you get driven out of your fort, that counts as a loss). Facing those brutal British charges gave the Americans badly needed confidence. They really could stand toe-to-toe with the British.

Washington Takes Command

"The liberties of the country are safe!"

That's what George Washington said when he heard the news from Bunker Hill. Like everyone else, he had been worried that untrained American volunteers would not stand their ground in the face of a fierce British attack. Now he knew better.

Then Washington got a look at his new Continental army. And he started worrying again.

Washington found about 20,000 men crowded into a stinky, dirty camp of tents and shacks. These guys were not used to doing laundry (they considered it women's work) so they just walked around in filthy, rotting clothes. There were serious shortages of guns, ammunition, and fresh food. And soldiers from different colonies were too busy fighting each other to think about attacking the British. That winter one snowball fight between soldiers from Massachusetts and Virginia exploded into a thousand-man fistfight. Washington personally plunged into the mess and started yanking people apart.

As he tried to discipline his army, Washington found himself giving some strange orders. "The general does not mean to discourage the practice of bathing while the weather is warm enough to continue it," Washington told his soldiers. "But he expressly forbids it at or near the bridge in Cambridge." Why is that, General?

"It has been observed and complained of, that many men, lost to all sense of decency and common modesty, are running about naked upon the bridge whilst passengers, even ladies of the first fashion in the neighborhood, are passing over it."

Yes, getting these guys to behave was going to be a real challenge.

Bored in Boston

Meanwhile, the British army was still bottled up in Boston. There was very little to eat that winter, and nothing to do. Lieutenant Martin Hunter remembered one way the men tried to

George Washington

fight the boredom. "Plays were acted twice every week by the officers and some of the Boston ladies," he said.

One night the British actors were about to put on a new "farce," or comedy—it was a play that made fun of Americans as clowns and cowards. British soldiers dressed up as Americans and got ready to take the stage.

The Americans knew about the play (thanks to those spies again). They decided to have some fun. Just as the show was about to start, American soldiers started firing at a British fort in town.

Inside the playhouse, one of the British actors (dressed as an American) ran on stage and shouted for silence. He announced that the rebels were attacking! But the audience started laughing—they thought this was part of the show.

"The whole audience thought that the sergeant was acting a part in the farce," Martin Hunter reported, "and that he did it so well there was a general clap, and such a noise that he could not be heard again for a considerable time."

The soldier kept shouting that this was a real attack. Finally realizing the danger, the audience members all stood up and started racing around in a panic, jumping over chairs, stepping on fiddles. The actors called out for water to wash the makeup off their faces. When they got out to the fort, they realized they had been tricked. The Americans were not really attacking Boston.

And Stay Out!

The next time it wasn't a trick.

On the morning of March 3, 1776, British general William Howe (who had taken over command from General Gage) pulled out his telescope and looked up at some nearby hills called Dorchester

Heights. He saw cannons pointing down at him. "These fellows have done more work in one night than I could make my army do in three months!" cried Howe.

Actually, it had taken more than one night to get those big guns in place. These were the cannons captured that May by Ethan Allen at Fort Ticonderoga. Washington had wanted the guns in Boston, so he sent Colonel Henry Knox to go get them. Knox was an enormous twenty-five-year-old bookstore owner who loved to read books about cannons. In the Continental army, that made Knox a cannon expert (they didn't have any real experts).

Using sleds and teams of oxen, Knox and his men pulled about sixty cannons three hundred miles from Fort Ticonderoga to Boston. Washington had them placed on Dorchester Heights.

Suddenly General Howe decided it was time to leave town. The truth is, it's no fun living in a city with huge guns pointing down at you. The British sailed out of Boston on March 17, 1776.

And they never came back.

When Washington happily reported the good news to Congress, he included a special note to John Hancock, whose Boston mansion had been used by British officers. "I have a particular pleasure in being able to inform you, Sir," wrote Washington to Hancock, "that your house received no damage worth mentioning. Your furniture is in tolerable order and the family pictures are all left entire and untouched."

The only bad news was that someone had stolen Hancock's backgammon set.

Independence Time?

A writer named Mercy Otis Warren celebrated the liberation of Boston by writing a new play called *The Blockheads*. It was a comedy about the British army in Boston, and she gave the British characters silly names like General Puff and Mr. Shallow. In the play, cowardly British officers were terrified of the Americans. Here's a sample:

> General Puff: *You see, gentlemen, our situation. Our enemies are gaining on us hourly! One night more perhaps will make us their prisoners!*
> Mr. Shallow: *Why will you desire us to go to battle? Are you for seeing another Bunker Hill . . . ?*

Mercy Otis Warren's good friend Abigail Adams was hoping there would be more good news to celebrate in 1776. She was convinced that it was time for the colonies to officially declare independence from Britain. In fact, she was wondering what her husband, John, and the other members of Congress were waiting for. "I long to hear that you have declared an independency," wrote Abigail. John replied:

> *"As to declarations of independency,*
>
> *be patient."*

How long would Abigail have to be patient? That's the next story.

John Adams

Declare Independence, Already!

Here's the big question of 1776: Are you for or against independence from Britain? You can put Benjamin Franklin down in the "for independence" column. After a lifetime of success as a writer, inventor, diplomat, and founder of colleges, libraries, fire departments, and about forty other things, Ben Franklin was the most famous American in the world. And now, going strong at age seventy, he was serving in Congress and urging the younger members (they were all younger) to make the break from Britain.

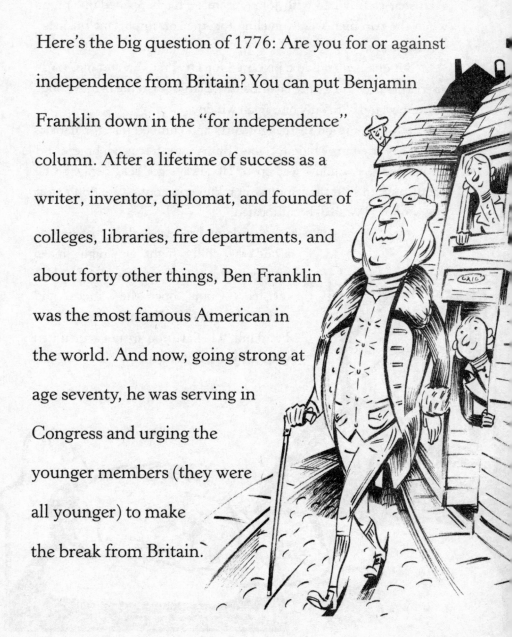

Anything for the Cause

Just how strongly did Benjamin Franklin feel about American independence? He would do almost anything for the cause— even share a tiny bed with John Adams. This happened one night when the two men were traveling together on important business for Congress.

"But one bed could be procured for Dr. Franklin and me," Adams explained, "in a little chamber little larger than the bed, without a chimney and with only one small window."

Both men put on their nightshirts and climbed into the narrow bed. They tried to get comfortable. But Adams felt a cool breeze and he noticed the window was open. He always got cold easily. So he jumped up to shut the window. Franklin cried out, "Oh, don't shut the window! We shall be suffocated!"

Adams tried to explain that he was afraid the chilly night air might make him sick. But this was nonsense, Franklin insisted. "Come, open the window and come to bed, and I will convince you," said Franklin. "I believe you are not acquainted with my theory of colds."

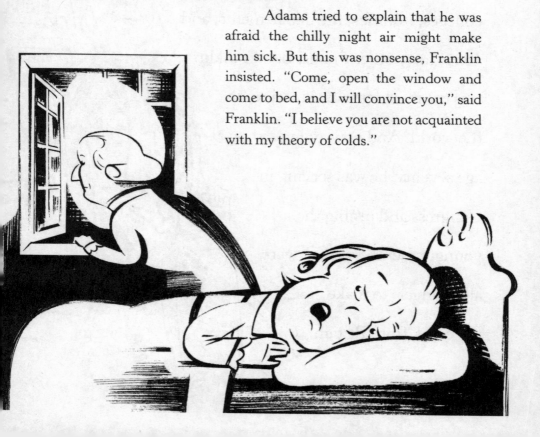

There was no point arguing with Franklin. So Adams left the window open, leapt back into bed, and pulled the covers up to his chin. Then Franklin began a very long lecture on air and breathing and the true causes of colds. . . .

To Adams, this was better than any bedtime story. "I was so much amused," Adams recalled, "that I soon fell asleep, and left him and his philosophy together."

Your Turn, Paine

So John Adams and Ben Franklin couldn't share a bed peacefully. But they could agree that it was time for the thirteen colonies to declare themselves a free and independent country. What about the other three million colonists? Many of them still weren't convinced that independence was such a great idea. After all, they were proud to be part of the British Empire. What would it be like to be an American citizen? No one really knew how that would turn out.

Thomas Paine, it's time for you to enter the story.

After spending his first thirty-seven years in Britain, Tom Paine sailed away from his homeland in 1774. He left behind several failed careers, two failed marriages, and a reputation as a clever but fairly annoying fellow. He was the kind of guy who would come over to your house and then stay for weeks, lazily lying around your living room and eating your food.

But when he felt like working, Paine had an amazing ability to write powerful and convincing arguments. He showed writing talent early in life, as you can see from this poem eight-year-old Tom wrote for his dead pet bird:

Here lies the body of John Crow,
Who once was high but now is low;
Ye brother Crows take warning all,
For as you rise, so must you fall.

When his boat arrived in Philadelphia, Paine was so sick from the journey that he had to be carried ashore on a stretcher. Not a good start. He recovered quickly, though, and soon found work writing for a few newspapers.

By early 1776, Paine was ready to write something big. Really big. He was sure the colonies should declare independence, and he wanted to convince Americans that they could make it on their own. So he published a pamphlet called *Common Sense*, which was filled with punchy lines like:

"The sun never shined on a cause of greater worth."

"In free countries the law ought to be King; and there ought to be no other."

"Everything that is right or reasonable pleads for separation."

"A government of our own is our natural right."

Common Sense was a wild success. "I believe the number of copies printed and sold in America was not short of 150,000," reported Paine with pride. George Washington soon noticed that Paine's writing was winning many Americans over to the side of independence. "I find *Common Sense* is working a powerful change in the minds of many men," he said.

After years of failure, Paine finally could have made some money. Instead, he donated his *Common Sense* profits to the Continental army. He asked that the money be used to buy mittens for the soldiers. "I did this to do honor to the cause," Paine said.

Abigail's Advice

Now it was March 1776, and Abigail Adams was still waiting for a declaration of independence. She and the Adamses' five children were living at the family house near Boston. Abigail wrote frequently to John in Philadelphia, keeping him up to date on their family and friends. "The little folks are very sick and puke every morning," she wrote in one letter. "But after that they are comfortable."

John wrote back with all the latest news from Congress. But his letters were always too short for Abigail—she wanted more information. "You justly complain of my short letters," John admitted. He said he was too busy to write more.

Abigail must have accepted this excuse, because she kept writing long letters to John. She knew that when the colonies declared independence, the new country would need a new government. And in a letter that later became famous, Abigail offered John some advice on what this government should be like:

"And by the way in the new code of laws which I suppose it will

Thomas Paine

be necessary for you to make I desire you would remember the ladies, and be more generous and favorable to them than your ancestors."

Why should John "remember the ladies"? You probably know that women had few rights in those days. They couldn't vote, run for elected office, or attend college. And married women had to give up control of all their property to their husbands. Suppose a woman owned a farm, for example. Once she was married, her husband could sell the farm without her permission!

Abigail was ready for some changes. She even warned John that women might start a revolution of their own:

"If particular care and attention is not paid to the ladies, we are determined to foment *a rebellion, and will not hold ourselves bound by any laws in which we have no voice, or representation."*

Abigail was joking with John, but she was also expressing a serious idea. Too bad John wasn't quite ready for Abigail's ideas. "As to your extraordinary code of laws, I cannot but laugh," he wrote to her.

Abigail Adams

*spark

King George Update

We haven't checked in on King George in a while. Do you miss him?

As you might expect, the king was not waiting around to hear any declarations of independence. In a speech to Parliament, George declared the American colonies to be in an official state of rebellion. The king called Patriot leaders "wicked and desperate persons" and vowed to "bring the traitors to justice."

To help get this done quickly, Britain needed more soldiers. So King George rented some from Germany. You can do that when you're a king. It worked like this: George paid German princes a lot of money, and the princes sent German soldiers to fight for Britain. And the princes actually got extra cash for every German soldier that was killed. You can do that when you're a prince.

In the spring of 1776 Americans started reading the shocking news: boats full of German soldiers were on their way west across the Atlantic Ocean! *How could King George do this?* colonists wondered. *How could he send foreign troops here to kill us?*

King George had been hoping to stop a revolution. Instead, he actually made more Americans think it was time to declare independence.

Congress Heats Up

And Congress needed the shove. Let's let a member of Congress named Joseph Hewes sum up the mood in Philadelphia: "Some among us urge strongly for independence . . . others wish to wait a little longer."

These were tense times in Congress. Members spent twelve

hours a day (often without snack breaks) meeting in the hot, stuffy Pennsylvania State House. Then, at night, they continued working and arguing in taverns and inns.

These guys were not only debating independence—they were trying to help run a war too. Like his cousin John, Samuel Adams hardly had time to keep in touch with his family. "I can scarcely find time to send you a love letter," Adams wrote to his wife.

By the middle of June, a majority of the members of Congress were finally ready to declare independence . . . almost. You can't just wake up one day and say, "Okay, now we're independent." You really need some kind of official declaration. You know, a written document that explains your reasons for becoming independent. What you need is a Declaration of Independence.

The members of Congress elected a five-man committee to write the Declaration: Roger Sherman, Robert Livingston, Benjamin Franklin, John Adams, and a young lawyer from Virginia named Thomas Jefferson. Jefferson was fairly new in Congress, and he hadn't spoken much so far. John Adams said of Jefferson: "The whole time I sat with him in Congress, I never heard him utter three sentences together."

No, Jefferson wasn't much of a public speaker. He could write, though. And he was about to do some pretty good writing.

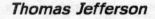

Thomas Jefferson

Who Gets the Job?

Who should write the Declaration of Independence? That was the committee's first decision. Franklin was sick in bed, so he was out. John Adams thought Thomas Jefferson was the man for the job. Jefferson wasn't so sure. According to Adams, he and Jefferson had a discussion that went like this:

Jefferson: *You should do it.*
Adams: *Oh! No.*
Jefferson: *Why will you not? You ought to do it.*
Adams: *I will not.*
Jefferson: *Why?*
Adams: *Reasons enough.*
Jefferson: *What can be your reasons?*
Adams: *Reason first—you are a Virginian, and a Virginian ought to appear at the head of this business. Reason second—I am obnoxious, suspected, and unpopular. You are very much otherwise. Reason third—you can write ten times better than I can.*
Jefferson: *Well, if you are decided, I will do as well as I can.*
Adams: *Very well. When you have drawn it up, we will have a meeting.*

John Adams

Writing at night in his room (after spending long days in Congress), Jefferson worked on the document for the next two weeks. When he had a draft he liked, he made a copy and sent it to Franklin, who was still stuck in bed. Franklin made a few quick suggestions. Then the document was given to Congress. "We were all in haste," John Adams explained. "Congress was impatient."

Just a Few Changes

Don't you hate it when you hand in a report and your teacher gives it back all marked up with corrections in red ink? Now you know how Jefferson felt on July 3, 1776. Jefferson sat in Congress, a look of pain on his face, as he watched the other members change his work. He was sure they were ruining some of the best parts.

Ben Franklin (who was finally feeling better) sympathized with the sensitive Jefferson. He sat down next to Tom and tried to distract him by telling him funny stories.

As Adams said, Congress was in a hurry. So by the next day, the members were ready to vote on Jefferson's document. Congress approved the Declaration of Independence on July 4, 1776.

Today, we think of this as the most important day in our country's history. To Jefferson, July 4 was just another day. He made only two entries in his diary that day. First, he wrote that the temperature in Philadelphia rose from sixty-eight degrees to seventy-six degrees. Second, he noted that he had bought seven pairs of women's gloves to take back to Virginia.

What Does it Say?

Let's get right to the point. The Declaration of Independence basically says three things, in this order:

1. *People are born with certain rights.*

2. *King George has taken those rights from us.*

3. *So we're forming our own country.*

Of course, Jefferson's words are a little better. Okay, a lot better. This is how he introduced the idea of rights that belong to all people:

"We hold these truths to be self-evident, that all men are created equal, that they are endowed by their creator with certain unalienable rights, that among these are life, liberty, and the pursuit of happiness."

Not bad. Then Jefferson went on to say some nasty things about King George: "The history of the present King of Great Britain is a history of repeated injuries . . . all having in direct object the establishment of an absolute tyranny over these states."

Thomas Jefferson

Jefferson listed all the ways King George had violated the colonists' rights. It was a very long list—we don't have room for it here.

Then he came to the part everyone was waiting for: "We, therefore, the representatives of the United States of America . . . declare that these united colonies are, and of right ought to be free and independent states."

And that's how you declare independence in style.

Sign Here—If You Dare

The Declaration of Independence was read in the streets and printed in newspapers. Pretty soon the whole country (we can call it a country now) was talking about it. Abigail Adams wrote to John, saying she looked forward to "the future happiness and glory of our country." She said she was very proud that her husband had been such a big part of founding a new nation.

John Adams was proud also. But he told Abigail that some of the other members of Congress were not too eager to sign their names to the Declaration of Independence. That's because anyone who signed it would be considered a traitor to Britain. And the punishment for traitors was well known: death by hanging.

This frightening fact was on everyone's mind when members gathered to sign the Declaration. John Hancock signed first, then had this exchange with Ben Franklin:

> John Hancock: *There must be no pulling different ways. We must all hang together.*
>
> Ben Franklin: *"Yes, we must indeed all hang together, or most assuredly we shall all hang separately."*

With this very real danger in mind, a tall, heavy member of Congress named Benjamin Harrison turned to a skinny member named Elbridge Gerry and said: "When the hanging scene comes to be exhibited, I shall have the advantage over you on account of my size. All will be over with me in a moment, but you will be kicking in the air half an hour after I am gone."

That was kind of a sick joke, but it captured the nervous mood in Congress. There was no turning back now.

United States of America

July 4, 1776

more Massachusetts (later became Maine)

Claimed by both New York and New Hampshire (later became Vermont)

New Hampshire

New York

Massachusetts

Rhode Island

Connecticut

Pennsylvania

New Jersey

Maryland

Delaware

Virginia

North Carolina

South Carolina

Georgia

"I am well aware of the toil, and blood, and treasure, that it will cost us to maintain this declaration, and support and defend these states."

—John Adams to Abigail

Bad Reviews in Britain

Copies of the Declaration of Independence were sent across the ocean to Britain. As far as we know, King George pretended it didn't exist. But lots of other British people did read the Declaration. Some were not very impressed. Their major complaint was this: many members of Congress were slave owners. How could slave owners declare that "all men are created equal"? How could people who own slaves say that all men have the right to "life, liberty, and the pursuit of happiness"?

Or, as a famous English writer named Samuel Johnson put it: "How is it that the loudest yelps for liberty come from the drivers of slaves?"

You've got a good point, Johnson. If you visited the homes of George Washington, Thomas Jefferson, Patrick Henry, and many other Patriot leaders, you would have seen enslaved African Americans. Did these guys believe in freedom, or didn't they? Patrick Henry wrestled with this question in a letter to a friend, saying:

"Would anyone believe I am the master of slaves of my own purchase? I will not, I cannot justify it."

Washington and Jefferson also wrote against slavery in their personal letters. But they simply did not see the American Revolution as a fight for the freedom of all Americans, black and white.

As you have figured out by now, the story of our country is not a fairy tale. No one is

Patrick Henry

perfect and not everyone lives happily ever after. Hey, at least it's not boring.

Remember That Statue?

By July 1776, George Washington and the Continental army had moved from Boston to New York City. On July 9, Washington had the Declaration of Independence read to his soldiers. They gave three loud cheers.

Then some of the guys went to the park in town where a King George statue was standing. This was the statue that New Yorkers had put up after the king agreed to repeal the Stamp Act. Now American soldiers helped a group of New York Patriots tie ropes around the top of the statue and yank it down to the ground. They even had an idea of how to reuse the statue's four thousand pounds of metal. "The lead we hear is to be run up into musket balls for the use of the Yankees," said a soldier named Isaac Bangs.

But General Washington knew he would need a lot more than a fancy declaration and bullets from a statue. The British army was about to begin a massive attack in New York. And Washington had no idea how he was going to stop it. He warned his men, "The eyes of all our countrymen are now upon us. The fate of unborn millions will now depend, under God, on the courage and conduct of this army . . . we have therefore to resolve to conquer or die."

No pressure, guys. Just save your country—or die trying.

Losing and Retreating in '76

Sixteen-year-old Joseph Plumb Martin still hadn't made up his mind. Was today the day he would enlist in the Continental army? "I thought I was as warm a Patriot as the best of them," Martin said. On the other hand, he wasn't exactly sure he was ready to risk getting shot. "I felt myself to be a real coward," he admitted.

Expect a Bloody Summer

Joseph Plumb Martin walked up to the table where a Continental army officer was seated. A bunch of Martin's friends were standing around the table, trying to get their courage up.

"Come—if you will enlist, I will," said one friend to another.

"You have long been talking about it." was the reply. "Come, now is the time."

Martin sat down at the table. The officer handed him enlistment papers and a pen. Martin dipped the pen in ink. He continued going back and forth in his mind . . . and then he signed his name.

Martin left his home in Connecticut and sailed to New York City to join George Washington's army. He began exercising and training. And he began eating army food. The flour-and-water biscuits were especially bad. "They were hard enough to break the teeth of a rat," Martin remembered.

Meanwhile, George Washington had troubles of his own. Washington had about 19,000 soldiers in New York. Most of them were like young Joseph—willing to fight, but totally inexperienced in battle. The British, on the other hand, had 32,000 well-trained troops. That included about 8,000 of those rented Germans, who were famously fierce fighters.

Washington knew he was in trouble. "We expect a very bloody summer at New York," he wrote to his brother. The general strapped two pistols to his belt and warned his men to stay ready. "I will not ask any man to go further than I do," he told them. "I will fight so long as I have a leg or an arm."

The soldiers slept in their uniforms, guns by their sides.

The British Are Coming!

The British attack came on August 22, a beautiful summer day in New York. Thousands of British and German soldiers poured off their boats and started marching toward the American forts on Long Island.

On their way to battle, British soldiers passed rows of apple trees, the branches bending with ripe, red fruit. This was too tempting a sight for guys who had been stuck aboard ships for months, eating salty, rotting ship food—so they stopped to pick and eat apples. Then they got right back to the attack.

Soon the soldiers approached the small village of Flatbush. And, as you might expect, the people of Flatbush began to panic. "Women and children were running hither and thither," said a sixteen-year-old girl named Femmetia. "Men on horseback were riding about in all directions." Femmetia looked down the street and saw the doors of the red schoolhouse fly open. "The boys rushed out with a shout," she said. No more school today!

Then Femmetia helped her mother and sister load everything they could carry into a wagon:

"My sister and I were all excitement,
rushing wildly about the house and
bringing the most useless things . . .
to put in the wagon. Mother coolly
took out whatever did not seem to
her necessary."

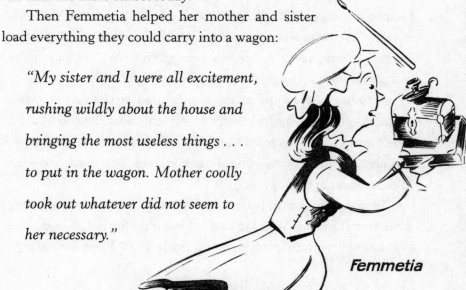

Femmetia

93

The family rode off to stay with relatives farther from the fighting. They came back to their village a few days later to inspect the damage. "Two of our neighbors' houses, as well as our own, were burned to the ground," Femmetia said.

A Midnight Escape

This battle was a disaster for the Continental army too.

In a week of fighting on Long Island, more than a thousand Americans were killed, wounded, or captured. And Washington's army was driven back, and back, and back . . . until it was right up against the edge of the one-mile-wide East River. Washington faced an ugly truth: his entire army was about to be captured right there, right then. Not exactly the way he was hoping the American Revolution would end. But could he slip out of the trap before it shut?

On August 29, Joseph Plumb Martin found out the army was moving when he saw the other soldiers of his company lining up and preparing to march. No one could tell him where they were going. First of all, they didn't know. Second of all, they weren't allowed to talk. "We were strictly enjoined [ordered] not to speak, or even cough," Martin said. "All orders were given from officer to officer, and communicated to the men in whispers."

As soon as it was dark, the men started crowding onto small boats. A group of Massachusetts fishermen under the command of John Glover rowed the boats back and forth across the river. (Glover's regiment, by the way, was one of the first to include black and white soldiers working side by side.)

To make the British believe that nothing special was happening, some American troops had to stay behind until the last second. They kept lots of campfires burning, which made it look like a normal night in the American camp. An officer named Benjamin Tallmadge remembered waiting all night for orders to march down to the river. "It was one of the most anxious, busy nights that I ever recollect," he said, "and being the third in which hardly any of us closed our eyes to sleep."

Glover and his men were still rowing back and forth across the river when the sun came up. Amazingly, fog saved them. A thick, wet fog settled over the river, and the entire army (including horses) escaped to Manhattan before the British knew what was going on. "In the history of warfare I do not recollect a more fortunate retreat," said Tallmadge.

Too bad you can't win wars by retreating.

The Story of Nathan Hale

The American army had escaped to Manhattan, but George Washington hardly felt safe. He knew the British would continue their attack very soon. But where? When? With how many men? Washington was desperate for any information about British plans. He needed a spy. Nathan Hale volunteered.

Nathan Hale was a twenty-two-year-old teacher who had no idea how to be a spy. One of Hale's friends from college, William Hull, tried to talk Hale out of accepting this dangerous mission. But Hale couldn't be budged. He said he had been in the army for a whole year and hadn't done anything yet. "I wish to be useful," he told his friend.

So Hale put on a plain brown suit, stuck his college diploma in his pocket, and entered British-controlled territory pretending to be a teacher in search of a job.

No one knows exactly what Hale did or where he went for the

next nine days. But on the night of September 21, some British soldiers became suspicious of Hale. They grabbed him and searched him and found more than just a college diploma. They found a map he had drawn and notes on the strength and location of the British army (a more experienced spy would have at least used invisible ink or secret codes).

Hale didn't even try denying that he was a spy. And the British didn't even bother giving him a trial. They hanged him the next morning.

When they put the rope around his neck, did Nathan Hale really say the famous line?

"I only regret that I have but one life to

lose for my country."

Yes he did, according to Hale's friend William Hull. Hull wasn't at the hanging, of course, but he got the story from a British officer who watched the execution.

And that's pretty much all we know about Nathan Hale.

More Bad News

Meanwhile, the Continental army was busy moving backward again.

As one of the soldiers in charge of guarding the shore of Manhattan, Joseph Plumb Martin kept a watch on the water. Every few

Nathan Hale

minutes he and the other American guards called to each other, "All is well!"

But the enemy ships were so close, British soldiers could hear the Americans talking. And when they heard the Americans say, "All is well!" they called back, "We will alter your tune before tomorrow night!" They kept their promise.

The British attacked again on September 15. And again the untrained Americans were forced to retreat. In the panic and confusion, Martin got separated from his unit. He was soon sprinting across the island of Manhattan, with the British army close behind. He dove into a swamp and hid behind bushes and weeds while the British marched past. "Several of the British came so near to me that I could see the buttons on their clothes. They, however, soon withdrew and left the coast clear for me again."

Washington stood on the battlefield watching his soldiers run for their lives. He screamed for the men to stop. He even hit a few of them as they passed, but the soldiers were simply too scared to stop running.

An American officer named George Weedon witnessed Washington's fury on this day. "The General," Weedon said, "three times dashed his hat on the ground, and at last exclaimed, 'Good God, have I got such troops as those!'"

Other witnesses heard Washington shouting: "Are these the men with whom I am to defend America?"

Washington was so angry, his officers had to pull him off the battlefield to keep him from getting captured.

Is This the End?

The Continental army continued fighting and retreating through October and November. The British chased them out of New York City, across the Hudson River, and south into New Jersey. "As we go forward into the country the Rebels fly before us," said British captain William Bamford. "'Tis almost impossible to catch them."

Things were looking terrible for Washington's army—what was left of it, that is. Soldiers were deserting every day. "Great numbers of them have gone off; in some instances almost by whole regiments," Washington reported to Congress.

To make things worse, men were taking Continental army guns and ammunition home with them. One guy even tried to take home a cannonball! When it was found in his bag, he had an excuse ready. He wanted to give it to his mother, he said. She could use it to pound spices.

By the end of November, Washington had just three thousand men left. This little army crossed the Delaware River and set up camp in Pennsylvania. Washington sent Congress an update, saying, "The situation of our affairs is critical and truly alarming." Congress agreed. With the British moving closer and closer to Philadelphia, the members of Congress decided to pack up and run away to Baltimore.

What else could go wrong? Plenty. Cold weather was coming and the soldiers had no winter clothing. And there was never enough to eat. Joseph Plumb Martin remembered the men in his unit going without food for two full days. When they complained of hunger pains, an angry officer reached into his pocket and pulled out a piece of dried corn that was burnt to a black crisp and said, "Here, eat this and learn to be a soldier."

Now for the worst part: Washington's small army was about to get even smaller. Most of the soldiers had enlisted in the army only until the end of the year. Then they expected to go home for the winter. Martin's enlistment ended in December, and he eagerly traveled home to his family and friends. "They appeared to be glad to see me," he said, "and I am sure I was really glad to see them."

Don't worry, Martin will be back in the army the next year. But Washington couldn't wait until the next year. "Ten days more will put an end to the existence of our army," he wrote on December 20.

Washington had ten days to save the Revolution.

Report from Trenton

Across the Delaware River from the American camp was the small town of Trenton, New Jersey. This was one of many towns now in the hands of the British army.

Guarding the town were about twelve hundred German soldiers. Americans called them "Hessians" because many of them came from the Hesse region of Germany. The Hessians took over most of the houses in Trenton and made themselves comfortable. "My friend Sheffer and I lodge in a fine house belonging to a merchant," wrote one officer.

This kind of invasion should get you out of school, right? Not if you went to Mistress Rogers's School for Young Ladies in Trenton, which stayed open all winter. We know this from letters that were sent to students that year. William Shippen, for instance, wrote to his daughter Nancy, age thirteen, saying:

"My dear Nancy: I was pleased with your French letter which was much better spelt than your English one, in which I was sorry to see four or five words wrong . . . Take care, my dear girl, of your spelling and your teeth."

And while most families got out of Trenton when the enemy arrived, a few stayed to try to protect their homes. A ten-year-old girl named Martha Reed stayed in town with her mother and younger brother—her father was off in the Continental army.

Martha later described the cold mid-December night that the enemy showed up at her door. "Mother and we two children were gathered in the family room," she said. "A great fire blazed in the chimney place . . . Suddenly there was a noise outside, and the sound of many feet. The room door opened and in stalked several strange men."

After warming up by the fire, the Hessian soldiers opened the storeroom and ate all the pickles and jarred vegetables. A bit later, they killed a hog and butchered it on the dinner table.

Even though Martha's mother spoke no German, she somehow managed to convince the soldiers that her husband was serving in the British army. So the Hessians agreed to let the Reeds stay in the house.

A few days later a child's coat gave the Reeds away. Martha explained: "To please my little brother, my mother had made for him an officer's coat of the rebel buff [gold] and blue, in which he delighted to strut and fight imaginary battles."

When the Hessians found this coat, they knew they'd been tricked. They were in the home of Patriots! "What a storm broke around us!" Martha said. "They shook the little coat in our faces, jabbering and threatening."

Martha's mother pulled the children outside and they all hid in the hen house—normally a bad hiding place, since chickens cluck and cackle when they're disturbed. Luckily, the soldiers had already eaten all the chickens.

Martha and her family spent a freezing and frightening night in the empty hen house. "That was a night I can never forget," she said.

The Lion in the Tub

In command of the German forces in Trenton was Colonel Johann "the Lion" Rahl. Bravery in battle earned Rahl his nickname. But he was also kind of a lazy guy. He liked to stay up late drinking and playing cards. Then he would sleep late and spend the rest of the morning in the tub.

"There were times," complained one of his officers, "when we would go to his quarters for the morning formation between ten and eleven o'clock and he would still be sitting in his bath."

Rahl was warned that the Americans might try to attack his army. He laughed and shouted, "Fiddlesticks! These clodhoppers will not attack us." Rahl knew the Americans were starving, freezing, and ready to go home.

He expected to enjoy a quiet winter at Trenton.

Across the River

The sun set at 4:35 on December 25. Christmas Day had been sunny and cold, about thirty-two degrees. Now clouds covered the stars and a miserable mixture of freezing rain and snow started falling.

Washington ordered his soldiers to pack sixty rounds of ammunition and a three-day supply of salted meat and bread. Sixteen-year-old John Greenwood was one of the many soldiers who wondered where the army was going that night. He was hoping he wouldn't have to march too far, because he was suffering from a horrible rash on his legs. Or, as he put it:

"I had the itch then so bad that my breeches stuck to my thighs, all the skin being off, and there were hundreds of vermin upon me."

At least Greenwood had shoes. Many of the men had worn through theirs and had to tie rags around their bare feet.

The soldiers gathered at the edge of the Delaware River. They saw black water clogged with bobbing, swirling chunks of ice. And they saw John Glover and his fishermen waiting to row them across the river.

The boats started crossing and re-crossing the water. It took many trips to get everyone over. Colonel Henry Knox (the cannon expert) was determined to get eighteen

John Greenwood

cannons over the river also. "The floating ice in the river made the labor almost incredible," he reported. "The night was cold and stormy; it hailed with great violence."

John Greenwood was one of the first to cross the river. Then he stood on the New Jersey side, waiting for hours. "It rained, hailed, snowed, and froze, and at the same time blew a perfect hurricane," he said. He and the other men pulled down fences and lit fires in a useless effort to keep warm. They watched the boats and waited.

Washington was watching and waiting too. "I have never seen Washington so determined as he is now," an officer named John Fitzgerald wrote in his diary. "He stands on the bank of the river, wrapped in his cloak, superintending the landing of the troops. He is calm and collected, but very determined."

The plan had been to get the army across the Delaware River by midnight. But thanks to the ice in the river, it took until three in the morning. Washington knew he would not be able to reach Trenton before dawn. "I determined to push on at all events," he said.

The army began the nine-mile march to Trenton.

Surprise!

You often read about weather being a major factor in historical events. This was definitely true of the Trenton attack. On most nights, the Hessians in Trenton sent soldiers out to patrol the roads leading into town. But the night of December 25 was just too cold and nasty. The routine patrol was canceled.

So Colonel Rahl and his men were quite surprised when Washington and the Americans marched into town at about eight o'clock in the morning. Hessian soldiers grabbed their guns and ran out into the street. By the time they figured out what was going on, though,

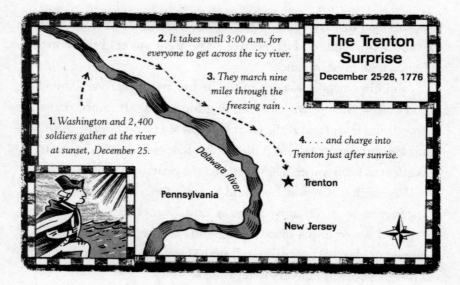

The Trenton Surprise
December 25-26, 1776

1. *Washington and 2,400 soldiers gather at the river at sunset, December 25.*

2. *It takes until 3:00 a.m. for everyone to get across the icy river.*

3. *They march nine miles through the freezing rain . . .*

4. *. . . and charge into Trenton just after sunrise.*

Delaware River

Pennsylvania

★ Trenton

New Jersey

Washington's men already had the town surrounded. And Henry Knox had his cannons set up and ready to go. "These, in the twinkling of an eye, cleared the streets," Knox reported.

There was absolutely nowhere for the Hessians to hide. They ran toward houses, but many of the women who had stayed in town suddenly stuck guns out the windows and starting firing.

The battle of Trenton was over quickly. Colonel Rahl was shot and killed. His entire army surrendered, except for a few men who managed to escape down the road. "This is a glorious day for our country," Washington told his officers.

And to make the day even better, American soldiers found lots of good stuff scattered around town. John Greenwood took a German sword as a souvenir. An American drummer threw his own drum away and picked up a much nicer German one. Other soldiers put on fancy brass German officers' hats and strutted around town.

Saved, for Now

After beating the Americans all year, British leaders in London had been sure they were about to win the war. "But all our hopes were blasted by that unhappy affair at Trenton," said George Germain, King George's top war advisor.

Washington wasn't done yet, though. He marched his troops to the town of Princeton and won another quick victory. These winter wins inspired thousands of new soldiers to join the army. The American Revolution was alive.

A Loyalist named Nicholas Cresswell was truly sorry to see the sudden change in the mood of Americans. "A few days ago they had given up the cause for lost," Cresswell said. "Their late successes have turned the scale and now they are all liberty-mad again."

But King George was still feeling confident. In fact, he had a new war plan. And he looked forward to crushing the Revolution in 1777.

Showdown at Saratoga

The British General John Burgoyne celebrated Christmas in 1776 by placing a bet on the American Revolution. Burgoyne wagered fifty golden guineas that he could beat the Americans and "be home victorious from America by Christmas Day, 1777." This was a bold bet. To win it, Burgoyne would have to cross the Atlantic, crush the Revolution, and get back to London—all in one year!

No Secrets Here

What made General John Burgoyne so confident about crushing the American Revolution? Two words: the plan. Burgoyne had spent the past few months working out a detailed plan for winning the war. He presented the secret strategy to King George. The king loved it.

So in the spring of 1777, Burgoyne loaded cases of champagne onto a ship (he always traveled in style) and set out across the ocean with high hopes.

General Burgoyne arrived in Quebec, Canada, in early May. As soon as he got off the boat, he started hearing people talk about his so-called secret strategy. The Quebec newspaper even had an article about it, describing exactly how Burgoyne planned to defeat the Americans! As usual in this war, neither side could keep anything secret.

Burgoyne was annoyed, but not discouraged. So the Americans knew his plan—so what? That didn't mean they could stop him.

The basic idea of the plan was simple: slice the United States in two. This would be done by attacking the centrally located state of New York from the north and south at the same time. Once the British controlled New York, all of New England would be cut off from the rest of the United States. The different regions wouldn't be able to help each other by sending soldiers or supplies back and forth. It would be like having an enemy's hands around your neck. The Revolution could be strangled.

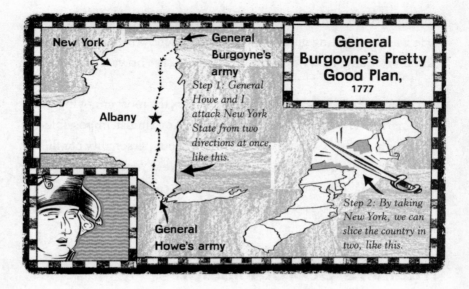

New York

General
Burgoyne's
army

**General
Burgoyne's Pretty
Good Plan,**
1777

*Step 1: General
Howe and I
attack New York
State from two
directions at once,
like this.*

Albany

*Step 2: By taking
New York, we can
slice the country in
two, like this.*

General
Howe's army

Benedict Arnold to the Rescue

Like everyone else, George Washington knew about Burgoyne's plan. But there was very little he could do. The British still had their main army, under the command of General William Howe, camped in and around New York City. Washington was worried that Howe would try to capture Philadelphia that year. So he had to keep his army nearby to prevent it. You can't just let the enemy capture your capital city, can you?

A separate American army, known as the Northern Army, would have to stop Burgoyne's invasion. Washington couldn't send many soldiers to the Northern Army, but he could at least send one of his top generals. He picked a former merchant from Connecticut named Benedict Arnold.

Arnold had already fought in many of the war's fiercest battles, and he was known for his attacking style and reckless bravery. Here's how one American soldier described Arnold's reputation in 1777: "He was our fighting general, and a bloody fellow he was. He didn't care for nothing; he'd ride right in. . . . He was as brave a man as ever lived."

True, Arnold was also known as perhaps the most annoying man in America. His loud, bossy style made him almost impossible to work with. But this was no time to worry about personality conflicts. Washington needed a fighter in northern New York, so he sent his best one. "We have one advantage over our enemy," Arnold said as he headed north. "It is our power to be free, or nobly die in defense of liberty."

Franklin's Secret Mission

Meanwhile, in Philadelphia, Ben Franklin packed up a lunch, climbed into a carriage with his two grandsons, and set off on a picnic. A picnic, Ben? At a time like this? Don't worry—it was part of a secret plan to help win the Revolution.

The plan was based on a simple fact, sad but true: the United States could not win this war without help. George Washington might win a small battle here and there, but the Continental army did not have enough soldiers, guns, and ships to defeat mighty Great Britain. What the Americans needed was a powerful ally. So Congress decided to try to persuade France to join forces with the United States. And Congress believed that seventy-one-year-old Ben Franklin was the man to do the convincing. Franklin was famous and highly respected in France—they just might listen to him.

But first Franklin had to actually get to France. And with British spies snooping around every corner in Philadelphia, this was going to be a dangerous trip. If the British found out about Franklin's plans, they would chase down his ship as it crossed the Atlantic Ocean. That would be the end of Ben Franklin.

So Franklin and his two grandsons (William, age seventeen, and Benjamin, seven) rode out of town on an innocent little picnic. Then, when they saw they hadn't been followed, they drove the carriage to a small port on the Delaware River. All three of them climbed onto a waiting ship.

Six weeks later, they were safely in France.

We'll Think About It

Battered and exhausted by the rough sea journey, Franklin had no time for rest. He and the boys jumped into a carriage and hurried toward Paris, the French capital. "The carriage was a miserable one," Franklin remembered, "with tired horses, the evening dark, scarce a traveler but ourselves on the road." And the dark road was far from safe.

"The driver stopped near a wood we were to pass through, to tell us that a gang of eighteen robbers infested that wood, who but two weeks ago had murdered some travelers on that very spot."

Benjamin Franklin

Luckily, Franklin managed to avoid the French bandits. But the British spies spotted him right away. David Stormont, the British ambassador to France, rushed a report to his bosses in London. "I learnt yesterday evening that the famous Doctor Franklin is arrived," wrote Stormont. "I cannot but suspect that he comes charged with a secret commission from the Congress. . . . In a word, my Lord, I look upon him as a dangerous engine."

A few days later, young William Franklin went on an errand for his grandfather. He went to the French foreign minister's office and delivered a letter stating that Benjamin Franklin was here in Paris to negotiate a treaty of friendship between the United States and France.

The official French reply was basically "Well . . . we'll think about it." Sure, King Louis XVI and friends were still bitter about losing the French and Indian War to their old enemy Britain. The French were definitely hungry for a little revenge. They didn't want to join this new war, though, unless they were sure the Americans could actually win it. And so far, the Americans had lost most of the big battles. French leaders decided to wait and see how the fighting went in 1777.

Franklin settled in for a long stay in France. He couldn't accomplish much until there was some good news from home.

Baroness von Riedesel

The News from Home

At first, there was no good news to report. Unless you were rooting for the British.

In July, General Burgoyne accomplished the first part of his plan: he captured Fort Ticonderoga from the Americans. This news delighted King George, who skipped into Queen Charlotte's bedroom, clapping and yelling, "I have beat them! Beat the Americans!"

The next step for Burgoyne's big army was to march about thirty miles from Fort Ticonderoga to the Hudson River. Things were going smoothly.

Baroness Frederika von Riedesel, for one, was having a wonderful time. Wife of the German general Friedrich von Riedesel, the baroness was one of hundreds of women who were traveling with Burgoyne's army (wives often went to war with their husbands in the 1700s). The baroness even brought her three young daughters along! As she wrote, this was an exciting opportunity for the family to see the world:

"When the weather was good we had our meals out under the trees, otherwise we had them in the barn, laying boards across barrels for tables. It was here that I had bear meat for the first time, and it tasted very good to me."

Then, just when everyone was having a fine time, the British started running into trouble. John Burgoyne (nicknamed "Gentleman Johnny" by his troops because he treated them well) insisted on living in luxury, even in the middle of a war. He needed thirty wagons just to haul all his champagne and fancy foods! This really slowed down the march, especially since the army was traveling over narrow paths through muddy, mosquito-filled forests.

And the Americans were doing a great job of making their British visitors feel unwelcome. American soldiers destroyed bridges and rolled boulders and logs into the road. They dammed up streams, causing them to flood the forest paths. Local farmers even burned their own crops, just to make sure the British wouldn't find anything to eat in New York.

Burgoyne was able to advance only one mile a day. By the beginning of September, his army was down to just a month's supply of food. And there was more bad news. You'll remember that Burgoyne's plan called for General William Howe to lead a second British army north from New York City. Now Burgoyne learned that Howe's army wasn't coming. General Howe had decided that he would rather attack Philadelphia than cooperate with Burgoyne's plan. (Howe didn't like Burgoyne. And since he outranked Burgoyne, he could do whatever he wanted.)

Gentleman Johnny was starting to sweat.

"When I wrote more confidently, I had not foreseen that I was to be left to pursue my way though such a tract of country and host of foes, without any cooperation from New York."

John Burgoyne

The leaves on the trees of northern New York were just starting to change from green to yellow and orange. To Burgoyne, the colorful leaves were a painful reminder that it was getting late in the year. If he was going to turn and march his army back to safety in Canada, he had to do it right then, before winter weather made the trip impossible.

Burgoyne thought about it . . . and decided to continue the attack. His army would try to fight its way south to Albany, where it could spend the winter indoors. "This army must not retreat," he told his men. Was he thinking about that bet he had made back in London?

A Little Help from Poland

The Americans knew that Burgoyne was coming. It was time to pick a spot and get ready for the showdown.

Benedict Arnold and a Polish military engineer named Thaddeus

Kosciusko got on their horses and started looking for the perfect place to fight. Kosciusko, or "Kos," as the Americans called him, was a new addition to the Continental army. Back in Poland, he had tried to elope (or run off to be married) with his girlfriend. But the woman's father caught the young couple and gave Kosciusko two choices: fight him in a duel or get out of Poland. Kos didn't want to kill the old guy, so he decided to leave his country. And as so many people have done since, he traveled to the United States in search of new opportunities. He met George Washington, and their conversation went like this:

Washington: *What do you seek here?*
Kos: *I come to fight as a volunteer for American independence.*
Washington: *What can you do?*
Kos: *Try me.*

Washington liked this guy's attitude (though he had terrible trouble spelling the name "Kosciusko"—he spelled it eleven different ways during the war). Washington sent Kos north to join the Northern Army.

An expert at designing and building forts near rivers, Kos was exactly what the Americans needed in September 1777. Kos and Arnold found a hill above the Hudson River near the town of Saratoga. This looked like a good place to try to stop Burgoyne. Kos took out his notebook and started sketching ideas for forts. They would have to be simple forts—the British army would be there in just a few days.

Pa-Pa Franklin

Back in France, Franklin eagerly opened every letter from home, hoping to read about a great American victory. But there had been no great victories yet. And to make things worse for poor Ben, he had to decode the letters before reading them. One letter began like this: "I am very glad that 105 is going to 156, and I am sure it will please 38 of 68."

This was a simple code, using numbers to stand for important people and places. Codes were necessary because Franklin was absolutely surrounded by British spies. He didn't know it at the time, but even his own personal secretary was selling information to the British! Still, Franklin hated working with codes. He found it boring.

Why were the British so interested in Ben Franklin's secrets? They were worried Franklin might be in France to do more than just work out a treaty. Franklin was world famous for his experiments with lightning and electricity, and there were wild rumors that Franklin was now in France to build some secret electrical machine that could destroy all of Britain. One British secret agent actually described Franklin's plan like this:

"He proposes to have a chain carried from Calais [France] to Dover [England]. He, standing in Calais, with a prodigious electrical machine of his own invention, will convey such a shock as will entirely overturn our whole island."

The truth is, Franklin was spending most of his time eating and drinking. The fancy people of Paris invited Franklin to parties every night, and he was too polite (and hungry) to refuse.

Everyone in France, it seemed, wanted to get a close-up look at Franklin's simple American clothes and his beaver-fur hat. Artists and sculptors gathered around to paint and sculpt his famous face. Young women lined up to kiss his cheek and call him "Pa-pa Franklin." Then they rushed to their wig makers and asked for wigs shaped like Franklin's fur hat. (This was called wearing your hair "à la Franklin.")

Franklin knew that most of this stuff was pretty silly. But he also knew that he wasn't wasting his time. Franklin's fame and popularity were actually powerful tools. One dinner party at a time, he was winning the French people over to the American cause.

If only the American army could help him out a little.

The Battle of Saratoga: Part One

Now back to New York.

After a week of sweaty work under a killer summer sun, the Americans completed a fort at Saratoga. And just in time, too—Burgoyne's army attacked the American fort on September 19, 1777. The battle of Saratoga was on.

Just before the attack began, a general named Horatio Gates arrived at Saratoga to take command of the Northern Army. Gates was a careful commander, a guy who didn't like to take chances. (Soldiers nicknamed him "Granny Gates" because the way he wore his glasses on the end of his nose made him look like an elderly woman.) Gates wanted to keep his army inside the fort and fight from behind the walls of earth and logs.

General Benedict Arnold disagreed. Arnold, who was second in command, wanted to charge out of the fort and fight in the woods and fields. As always, Arnold made his opinions known to everyone. So he and Gates argued for a while. Finally, Gates got so annoyed that he gave Arnold permission to take some soldiers out to fight.

This turned out to be a very important decision, because it ruined the British battle plan. Burgoyne had been planning to roll his cannons right up to the American fort. Instead, the two armies crashed into each other in a field surrounded by forests. The Americans used the trees to their advantage, climbing up to high branches and firing their rifles down on the British with deadly accuracy.

The deafening blasts of guns and cannons continued all afternoon, making soldiers on both sides feel like they were stuck in the center of a nonstop thunderstorm. "Such an explosion of fire I never had any idea of before," said a young British lieutenant named William Digby. An American officer named Roger Lamb agreed: "Both armies seemed to be determined on death or victory."

As usual, Benedict Arnold was out in front of his men, charging right at the enemy guns. "Arnold rushed into the thickest of the fight with his usual recklessness, and at times acted like a madman," reported an American general named Enoch Poor. Arnold's fellow soldiers weren't sure if Arnold was very brave or very insane. Some thought he must be drunk. (There's no evidence that he was.)

Back in the British camp, Baroness von Riedesel listened to the battle with horror. "I shivered at every shot," she said, "for I could hear everything." She watched as the wounded men were carried back to camp, terrified that her husband would be among them. He wasn't.

Only darkness ended the fighting that day. Though more than one thousand men had been shot, neither side had won the battle. The exhausted armies collapsed and rested.

The Battle of Saratoga: Part Two

This battle left Burgoyne in serious trouble. He lost many of his best officers, and his army was nearly out of food. He wanted to try attacking the Americans one more time, but his soldiers were too tired. Still, he absolutely refused to retreat.

Meanwhile, in the American camp, the uneasy relationship between generals Gates and Arnold exploded. Gates wrote his official report to Congress on the battle of September 19. Even though Benedict Arnold had led much of the fighting that day, Gates didn't bother mentioning Arnold's name in the report.

Arnold stormed into Gates's tent, accusing Gates of jealousy and disrespect. Gates calmly responded by removing Arnold from command. Gates ordered Arnold to go to his tent and stay there.

Now a series of tense days and nights followed. By day, the Americans kept a constant watch for the attack they knew must be coming. By night, they were haunted by the barks and cries of hungry wolves that gathered in packs to scratch up the shallow battlefield graves. Wolves dragged out the bodies and . . . well, you can imagine. It was a rough three weeks.

Then, on October 7, the British attacked again. The top American officers raced to General Gates to get his battle orders. When Gates started naming the soldiers he wanted to send into battle, Benedict Arnold (who was supposed to be in his tent) interrupted with his opinion:

Arnold: *That is nothing. You must send a stronger force.*
Gates: *General Arnold, I have nothing for you to do. You have no business here.*

Arnold spat out a series of unprintable curses as he walked back to his tent. He paced back and forth for a while, listening to the sounds of the gunfire. Then he just couldn't take it anymore. He jumped on his horse and rode toward the battle, shouting,

"Victory or

death!"

Gates ordered him to come back. But Arnold was already gone.

Out on the battlefield, American soldiers cheered when they saw Arnold coming. Arnold rode all over the battlefield, leading charges and driving British and German soldiers backward. During one charge, he was shot in the leg and fell from his horse. "Rush on, my brave boys!" he called from the ground.

And the Americans did rush on. This time they won a clear victory over the British.

Benedict Arnold

Johnny Loses the Bet

Now Burgoyne's only hope was to try to escape before the Americans attacked again.

Baroness von Riedesel and her daughters climbed into a wagon and headed north. "We had been warned to keep extremely quiet," she remembered. "Thus we drove on all through the night. Little Frederika was very much frightened, often starting to cry, and I had to hold my handkerchief over her mouth to prevent our being discovered."

While all this was happening, a second British army finally got around to helping Burgoyne. General Henry Clinton led British soldiers north up the Hudson River, capturing some American forts.

A British messenger named Daniel Taylor hurried toward Burgoyne with the good news. Taylor was spotted by the Americans while traveling north, however, and just before he was captured he was seen to pull something out of his pocket and swallow it. The Americans forced Taylor to drink a nasty potion, which caused him to throw up—and out shot a silver bullet. Taylor tried to grab the bullet and swallow it again, but the Americans snatched it first. They unscrewed the hollow bullet, and inside was a note from General Clinton.

Obviously, Burgoyne never saw that note. And by October 17, Burgoyne's army was out of food. They could go no further. Gentleman Johnny took off the uniform he had been wearing for the past sixteen days and put on a clean one. He wanted to look nice when he surrendered to the Americans.

More than 5,700 British and German soldiers marched out to surrender. Trailing behind them were the pets they had picked up during their stay in the forests of New York, including foxes, raccoons, deer, and one black bear. "Thus ended all our hopes of victory, honor, glory," said the British lieutenant William Digby. Digby said that if he had been alone, he would have burst out crying.

Some of the British felt even worse when they got a close look at the army that had just whipped them. "Not one of them was properly uniformed," said a British soldier of the Americans, "but each man had on the clothes in which he goes to the field, the church or to the tavern."

No, the American soldiers didn't have fancy uniforms. But at Saratoga they gained something much more valuable: their first major victory over the British.

Ben Seals the Deal

"The news of Burgoyne's surrender lifted us up to the stars," wrote John Adams. Wait till Ben Franklin finds out.

In early December, a carriage pulled up to Franklin's house in France. Franklin had been hearing rumors that General Howe had captured his hometown of Philadelphia. Franklin rushed up to the messenger:

Franklin: *Sir, is Philadelphia taken?*
Messenger: *It is, sir. But sir, I have greater news than that. General Burgoyne and his whole army are prisoners of war!*

Burgoyne, a prisoner of war! This changed everything. After months and months of avoiding Franklin, France's King Louis and his officials finally agreed to work out a treaty with the United States.

Franklin prepared for his big meeting with King Louis by hiring the best wig maker in Paris (no one showed up to see the king without a nice wig). Unfortunately, the wig maker made Franklin a wig that didn't fit. A Paris newspaper reported the scene:

> Franklin: *Perhaps your wig is too small?*
> Wig maker: *No, your head, sir, is too big!*

The newspaper reporter added his own comment: "It is true that Franklin does have a fat head. But it is a great head."

Anyway, Franklin decided to go to the palace in his plain brown suit and his plain bald head. The king's servants were horrified (at first, they didn't even want to let him into the palace). Everyone waited, too scared to breathe, as Franklin boldly stepped up to meet King Louis. Luckily, Louis didn't seem to care about Franklin's head one way or the other. He simply looked at Franklin and said:

> *"Assure Congress of my friendship.*
> *I hope this will be for the good*
> *of the two nations."*

And that was that. Franklin's mission was accomplished.

King Louis XVI

The Turning Point

Now you can see why the battle of Saratoga is called the "turning point" of the American Revolution. The Continental army had won its biggest victory yet over the British. And this victory convinced France, one of the most powerful nations in the world, to join forces with the United States.

The members of Congress were so excited, they gave General Gates a special medal to celebrate the battle of Saratoga. And at night, members and their wives did a new dance called "the Burgoyne surrender."

Not everyone was dancing, though. Stuck in a hospital bed in Albany, Benedict Arnold was recovering very slowly from his wound. Army surgeon James Thacher reported: "Last night I watched with the celebrated General Arnold, whose leg was badly fractured by a musket-ball while in the engagement with the enemy. . . . He is very peevish, and impatient under his misfortunes."

It wasn't just the pain in Arnold's leg that was bothering him. He was tortured by the fact that Gates was getting the glory he felt belonged to him.

We'll be hearing more from Benedict Arnold.

Will We Ever Win This War?

In 1777, Joseph Plumb Martin, now seventeen, decided to rejoin the Continental army. He agreed to serve until the end of the war. "The general opinion of the people was that the war would not continue three years longer," Martin said.

Don't tell Joseph, but the American Revolution was going to last six more years.

A Long Way from Victory

Sure, the Americans had won that great Saratoga victory. But the British were still determined to smash this revolution. And they still had thousands of soldiers in the United States. In fact, they had thousands of soldiers in the *capital* of the United States. In September 1777 (while Burgoyne was fighting in New York) the main British army, under the command of General William Howe, captured the city of Philadelphia. Members of Congress packed very quickly and escaped to York, Pennsylvania.

Now the winter of 1777 approached, and George Washington was facing the same old maddening problems: lack of soldiers, lack of food, lack of clothing . . . "The army was now not only starved but naked," said Joseph Plumb Martin. "The greatest part were not only shirtless and barefoot, but destitute of all other clothing, especially blankets."

No, the Americans were nowhere near winning this war.

Terrible Times at Valley Forge

Washington decided to keep his army close to Philadelphia that winter. He wanted to make sure General Howe didn't make any sudden, unexpected moves. So in December 1777, 11,000 American soldiers marched toward a place called Valley Forge, about twenty miles west of Philadelphia.

Some of the men were so exhausted by the march, they leaned on their guns and slept standing up. Others were more worried about their aching feet. Dr. James Thacher reported, "It was not uncommon to track the march of the men over ice and frozen ground, by the blood from their naked feet."

There wasn't much at Valley Forge—just some bare trees and windy hills covered with frost and dead grass. Since some kind of shelter was needed, Washington ordered the men to build log cabins. Twelve soldiers would live in each cabin. The men who knew how to build log cabins finished theirs in two days. Then they helped the city boys, who had no idea how to build a house out of logs.

Washington knew his army was facing a dangerously long, hard winter. Martha Washington, who came to stay at Valley Forge, could see the concern on her husband's face:

"The General is well, but much worn with fatigue and anxiety. I never knew him to be so anxious as now."

Martha and the other women in camp knitted socks and shirts as fast as they could. And the men badly needed the clothing. Some had nothing but ragged summer clothes, and they could be seen dashing from hut to hut wrapped in blankets. When soldiers were on duty, they stood on their hats to keep their bare feet from freezing solid in the snow. When they weren't on duty, they shivered in their cabins, coughing from the smoke from their fires and trying to ignore the hunger pains in their bellies.

Martha Washington

Dr. Albigence Waldo described life at Valley Forge in a few harsh statements:

"I am sick—fatigue—nasty clothes—nasty cookery—vomit half my time—smoked out of my senses—the Devil's in it—I can't endure it—Why are we sent here to starve and freeze?"

The only one who had anything nice to say about Valley Forge was a young soldier named Richard Wheeler. "We are very comfortable and are living on the fat of the land," wrote Richard to his mother. Richard wasn't quite telling the truth—he just didn't want his mom to worry.

And she would have worried had she known that there was so little food at Valley Forge that horses were starving to death and dropping dead in the middle of camp. Men, also starving, were too weak to bury the heavy horses. "The carcasses of dead horses are lying in and near the camp," complained Washington. The rotting horse bodies stank up the camp and helped spread disease among the weakened soldiers.

An increasingly desperate and angry George Washington watched

Albigence Waldo

more than 2,500 soldiers die from cold, hunger, and disease at Valley

Forge. He was furious with Congress for not doing more to supply the army. And he knew that if the British chose this moment to attack, his army would be ruined.

The Good Life in Philadelphia

Luckily for the American Revolution, General William Howe preferred to spend the winter indoors.

Howe and the other top British officers sat by blazing fires, playing cards and sipping wine. The British had taken over all the finest houses in town, including Ben Franklin's three-story brick mansion. So Ben's daughter Sarah had to find a new place to live. "I shall never forget or forgive them for turning me out of house and home in the middle of winter," Sarah wrote to her father.

At least they wouldn't be able to steal Ben's books. "Your library we sent out of town, well packed in boxes," Sarah added.

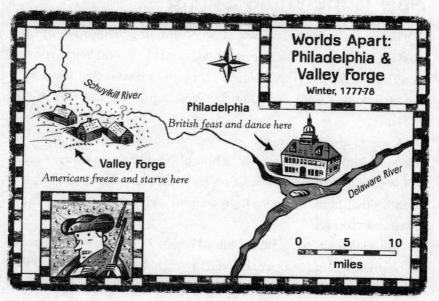

Worlds Apart: Philadelphia & Valley Forge
Winter, 1777-78

Schuylkill River

Philadelphia
British feast and dance here

Valley Forge
Americans freeze and starve here

Delaware River

0   5   10
miles

One of the British officers enjoying the Franklin mansion was a twenty-eight-year-old captain named John André. A talented artist, musician, and writer, André turned a local warehouse into a theater and put on thirteen different plays that winter. In his free time, he visited the homes of young American women, entertaining them by playing flute and reciting poetry.

André was a frequent guest at the Shippen home, where a beautiful and intelligent seventeen-year-old named Peggy Shippen lived with her wealthy family. John and Peggy sat in the living room for hours at a time, chatting and drinking tea (sometimes fifteen cups per visit). John took Peggy out to dinners and balls and on sleigh rides.

We don't know what they were talking about all this time. We do know that they soon started working together on a plan they hoped would destroy the American Revolution. Remember their names.

New Hope in the Spring

Back in Valley Forge, life was slowly beginning to improve. Spring brought warmer weather, and wagons full of food began rolling into the American camp. Soldiers set up their own little theater and put on plays—George and Martha Washington were always in the audience.

George also relaxed by tossing a ball back and forth with his officers. While Washington was a humble man, he was always proud of his strong right arm. "I have several times heard him say," said a friend, "that he never met any man who could throw to so great a distance as himself."

Another welcome sight at Valley Forge was a short, loud German fellow by the name of Friedrich von Steuben. Steuben impressed the Americans by telling them he had been a general in Germany. In fact, he had been a pretty low-ranking officer. He was very valuable to Washington, though, because he had years of experience training soldiers. And since most of the American volunteers had come straight from farms or workshops, they didn't know much about what soldiers were supposed to do.

Steuben got up at three in the morning each day to begin work. He broke the soldiers into small groups, personally showing each group how to work together in battle. The only problem was, he didn't speak much English. When soldiers misunderstood Steuben's commands, he often exploded into red-faced fits of shouting and cursing. First he cursed in German, then in French. Finally, he called to his translators:

"My dear Walker and my dear Duponceau, come and swear for me in English. These fellows won't do what I bid them."

The men laughed. Then they tried the exercise again. And again, and again. Joseph Plumb Martin, who was one of the many soldiers trained by Steuben that spring, noticed that the men seemed to have a new energy and confidence. They were eager to get out of Valley Forge and win some battles in 1778.

Friedrich von Steuben

Back in Action

In June 1778, the British army marched out of Philadelphia under the command of General Henry Clinton (General Howe had gotten sick of the war and decided to go home). The British had enjoyed the capital city, but now it was time to get back to the business of attacking Americans.

On his way out of town, John André stole everything he could carry from Ben Franklin's house, including scientific instruments and a large painting of the famous American.

Washington was ready for a fight himself. And on a scorching-hot day in late June, the Americans attacked Clinton's army in Monmouth, New Jersey.

In spite of the high hopes, this was another disappointing day for George Washington. He had made the mistake of putting a general named Charles Lee in charge of leading the attack. Lee was famous for his strange habits, including wearing filthy clothes and bringing his dogs to fancy dinner parties.

When the battle began, Lee decided not to follow Washington's plan (Lee considered himself to be much smarter than Washington). Lee attacked for a little while, then ordered the army to retreat. The soldiers stood around, wondering what to do next. That's when a furious Washington rode up, and this conversation was heard:

Washington: *General Lee! What are you about?*
Lee: *Sir?*
Washington: *I desire to know, sir, what is the reason for this disorder and confusion?*
Lee: *The American troops would not stand the British bayonets.*
Washington: *You damned poltroon [coward]—you never tried them!*

It was the only time American officers ever heard George Washington swear. So you know he was pretty mad.

While Washington tried to organize his soldiers, the temperature soared to one hundred degrees. As they did in many battles, brave women earned the nickname "Molly Pitcher" by carrying pitchers of water to men on the battlefield. Soldiers needed the water to cool down their blazing cannons (and to drink, of course).

One of the most famous "Molly Pitchers" was Mary Ludwig Hays. She dodged bullets at Monmouth to deliver water to her husband's cannon crew. When Mary's husband fainted from the heat, she stepped up to his cannon and started blasting it at the British. Joseph Plumb Martin saw the whole thing: "A cannon shot from the enemy passed directly between her legs without doing any other damage than carrying away all the lower part of her petticoat."

Like so many American Revolution battles, this one had no clear winner. And by the end of 1778, the Americans were no closer to winning the Revolution.

General Lee, by the way, was kicked out of the Continental army for disobeying orders. "Oh, that I were a dog, that I might not call man my brother!" he cried.

Are You the Famous Adams?

While Washington tried to think of a way to win the war, John Adams sailed to France.

The French had already begun sending soldiers, clothing, and weapons to the United States. But Congress hoped to get even more from France. Adams's new assignment: join Ben Franklin in Paris and help persuade the French to send more stuff to the Continental army.

John had wanted Abigail to come along, but he was afraid his ship might be captured by the British. So Abigail stayed home. As always, John and Abigail kept in touch through letters. "To tell you the truth," John wrote soon after arriving in France, "I admire the ladies here. Don't be jealous. They are handsome and very well educated."

Unfortunately, the French people quickly ruined John's good mood. They rushed up to him and asked, "Are you the famous Adams?" They knew all about the great revolutionary leader Samuel Adams. John had to say no, that's my cousin, I'm John Adams. The French had never heard of anyone by that name.

That was just the start of John's troubles. Adams had decided he could save his country some money by moving in with Ben Franklin. And just like the time they shared a bed in the crowded inn, John and Ben began arguing right away. For one thing, Adams complained, Franklin slept too late and spent too much time going to parties. Adams was also annoyed by the constant stream of visitors to their apartment—it seemed like everyone in France wanted to meet Benjamin Franklin. He told Abigail:

John Adams

"By far the greater part were women and children, come to have the honor to see the great Franklin, and to have the pleasure of telling stories about his simplicity, his bald head and scattering straight hairs."

The older, wiser Franklin tried to be patient with his roommate. "John Adams is always an honest man, often a wise one," Franklin said, "but sometimes and in some things absolutely out of his senses."

What Adams didn't realize was that Franklin knew exactly what he was doing. By forming close friendships with important people in Paris, Franklin was able to win favors for the Americans. For example, he succeeded in talking the French into giving a few of their old ships to the new Continental navy. Franklin made sure that one of the ships went to a captain he admired, a man from Scotland named John Paul Jones.

The Adventures of John Paul Jones

John Paul Jones had spent the past few years cruising the waters around Britain, capturing one British ship after another. Jones's favorite targets were British trading ships, which were loaded with valuable goods. After capturing these ships, Jones sailed them to nearby ports, sold the goods, and split the profits with his crew. Basically, he was a pirate. But this was legal in the 1700s. If you were at war with another country, you were allowed to capture any ship flying their flag (and you called yourself a privateer, not a pirate).

By 1778 Jones was the most feared captain in the American navy. Abigail Adams heard so much about his bold fighting style, she expected him to be a fire-breathing giant. She was surprised to meet the short (just over five feet), gentle-looking Jones. Abigail commented: "I should sooner think of wrapping him up in cotton wool and putting him in my pocket, than sending him to contend with cannon balls."

The British, of course, felt a bit differently about Jones—they were dying to catch and hang him. And on a warm night in September 1779, with moonlight reflecting off the smooth sea, they got their chance. A British warship named the *Serapis* spotted an American ship.

"What ship is that?" called out Richard Pearson, captain of the *Serapis*. "Answer immediately, or I shall be under the necessity of firing into you."

The next thing Pearson knew, a cannonball was flying toward his ship. Pearson had run into the *Bonhomme Richard,* under the command of John Paul Jones. Floating so close that they sometimes crashed together, the two ships battered each other with cannonballs, guns, and grenades. Both crews had to stop fighting every few minutes to put out fires on their wooden ships. Seeing that the *Bonhomme Richard* was badly damaged, Captain Pearson asked John Paul Jones if he was ready to surrender.

Jones barked back one of the best lines in American history:

"I have not yet begun to fight!"

The fighting continued for nearly four hours, and the *Bonhomme Richard* was soon blasted so full of holes that British cannonballs sailed in one side of the ship and out the other without hitting anything.

John Paul Jones

Then Jones saw one of his sailors, William Hamilton, do something amazing. "This brave man, on his own accord, seized a lighted match and a basket of grenades," Jones said. Hamilton climbed up the mast and started tossing grenades down onto the deck of the British ship. One of these grenades landed in a pile of gunpowder on the *Serapis*, sparking a massive explosion.

"It was awful!" reported British officer Francis Heddart. "Some twenty of our men were fairly blown to pieces. There were other men who were stripped naked, with nothing on but the collars of their shirts and wristbands."

The British pulled down their flag—the signal for surrender.

Jones had won, though his ship was so badly damaged, it sank two days later. And Jones himself was shaken by his violent victory. "A person must have been an eyewitness," he said, "to form a just idea of the tremendous scene of carnage, wreck and ruin that everywhere appeared."

Benedict Arnold in Love

Now we return to the never-boring Benedict Arnold. Nearly a year after the battle of Saratoga, Arnold had still not recovered from his wounds. Splinters from his shattered bone often poked into the nerves in his left leg, causing unbearable pain. Clearly, Arnold was not well enough to charge around the battlefield on horseback. So Washington gave him the fairly easy job of protecting Philadelphia.

Arnold had not been in town long before he met and fell in love with . . . guess who? Young Peggy Shippen! Peggy easily accomplished something British guns had not—she made the great general nervous. Arnold wrote:

"Twenty times have I taken up my pen to write to you, and as often has my trembling hand refused to obey the dictates of my heart."

Arnold got over his fears, though, and soon he won Peggy's heart. They were married in April 1779 (he was thirty-nine; she was nineteen).

You might think Benedict Arnold would finally be happy. Aside from the pain in his leg, though, he was still bitter about seeing Horatio Gates take credit for his victory at Saratoga. Arnold was the kind of guy who always felt people didn't appreciate him enough. Also, Arnold was broke. He had recently borrowed a fortune to buy Peggy a huge house, and he had no hope of paying back the loan.

Just a month after his marriage, Benedict Arnold decided to see how much the British would pay him to change sides in the war.

Peggy, a Loyalist at heart, played a key role in Benedict Arnold's secret plan. She knew that he would need to begin sending messages to the British, so she helped him contact her good friend John André. André was now an assistant

Benedict Arnold

to General Clinton—in a perfect position to help with the plot. In a long series of coded letters written in invisible ink, the three started working out their strategy.

Arnold's Fiendish Plan

In the summer of 1780, Benedict Arnold took over command of West Point, an American fort on the Hudson River in New York. Control of West Point was so important, Washington called it "the key to America." It was also the key to Arnold's plan.

Here's how it was supposed to work. Arnold and André would agree on a time for the British to attack West Point. Arnold would make sure to have his soldiers in all the wrong places, and the British would capture the fort easily. And there was more. George Washington was coming to inspect West Point in September. If the British timed their attack just right, they could grab General Washington too! In exchange, Arnold was to be paid a cool 20,000 pounds and made a general in the British army.

One of the most amazing things about Benedict Arnold's plot is just how close it came to working. Imagine how different our history would be if Washington had been taken to Britain and hanged! Arnold made a critical mistake, though. He insisted on meeting André face-to-face, so the two men could work out the last-minute details of their plan.

At about two in the morning on September 22, André rowed a small boat to a dark spot on the shore of the Hudson River. Arnold was waiting for him.

André Is Captured

Arnold and André talked until sunrise. Arnold wrote out plans showing just how the British should attack West Point. André put the papers in his boot, got on a horse, and rode south toward New York City (which the British still controlled). There he would meet with General Clinton, and then the British attack could begin.

One big problem: the woods north of New York City were a dangerous "no man's land"—an area in between British and American territory, filled with gangs of violent bandits. Some gangs were pro-American, some pro-British, but mostly they just liked to steal people's money.

As André rode through these woods, three men jumped out from behind a tree and grabbed his horse. André had a split second to guess which side these guys were on. He guessed wrong:

André: *I am glad to see you. I am an officer in the British service.*
Bandit: *Get down. We are Americans.*

Struggling to keep his cool, André instantly changed his story. He tried to frighten the thieves by saying he was actually an American on urgent business for General Arnold: "Gentlemen, you had best let me go or you will bring yourselves in trouble, for, by stopping me, you will detain the general's business."

But these guys just wanted to know one thing: "Where is your money?"

"Gentlemen, I have none about me," André explained.

The men pulled André off the road and searched him. And André really didn't have much money on him. But he did have some very strange papers stuffed in his boot. The thieves started reading the papers. . . .

And Arnold Escapes

Back at West Point, Arnold was eating breakfast at his headquarters when a messenger dashed in and handed over an urgent note. Arnold tore it open and read: a British spy was just captured with maps of West Point in his boot!

Arnold leapt up from the table, ran upstairs as fast as his bad leg would carry him, and told Peggy the terrible news (she was in bed with their newborn son, Edward). Then he hobbled outside, raced his horse down to the river, hopped on a boat, and started rowing south.

That was the last time anyone saw Benedict Arnold in an American uniform.

At that very moment, George Washington and his staff were approaching Arnold's headquarters. The men were all looking forward to seeing the famously beautiful Peggy. "You young men are all in love with Mrs. Arnold," Washington teased his officers.

But as the boat approached Arnold's house, it started to seem like something wasn't right. Arnold should have fired a few cannons as a salute to the commander in chief. But the cannons were silent. "The impropriety [incorrectness] of his conduct when he knew I was to be there struck me very forcibly," Washington later said. "But I had not the least idea of the real cause."

Just minutes later, he learned the real cause. As Washington was sitting down to lunch in Arnold's house, another messenger ran in and handed over the papers found in John André's boot. They were maps and plans for attacking West Point—all in Benedict Arnold's handwriting!

Washington sat quietly for a moment, holding the papers in shaking hands. He finally looked up at General Henry Knox and said, "Arnold has betrayed me. Whom can we trust now?"

Washington soon shook off the shock and went to work. He got the soldiers at West Point ready for a British attack (though none came). Then he put John André on trial, found him guilty of being a spy, and hanged him. Washington would much rather have hanged Arnold, but Arnold was beyond his reach, safe in British headquarters in New York City.

Peggy, meanwhile, managed to save her skin with a brilliant bit of acting. When Washington came to her room, Peggy threw a hysterical fit, shouting over and over, "That is not General Washington! That is the man who is going to kill my child!" She was so shocked by her husband's treason, it seemed, that she had lost her senses! Washington was convinced that she had nothing to do with the plot.

Peggy later joined her husband in New York.

No End in Sight

Once again, Washington had just barely escaped disaster. And while that was something to be grateful for, the entire country was getting sick and tired of this war. The American Revolution entered its seventh year in 1781, with no end in sight. The government didn't even have enough money left to pay its soldiers.

One day in February, Washington was walking up the stairs at his headquarters. Halfway up the staircase, he met his twenty-year-old assistant, Alexander Hamilton, who was coming down. Washington told Hamilton he needed help right away with some important papers.

"I answered that I would wait on him immediately," Hamilton later said.

Washington went to his office and sat down. He waited. No Hamilton. Washington stepped out into the hall and started pacing back and forth above the staircase. His impatience turned to anger, and his anger bubbled toward the boiling point. Finally, he spotted Hamilton at the bottom of the stairs.

Washington: *"Colonel Hamilton, you have kept me waiting at the head of the stairs these ten minutes. I must tell you, sir, you treat me with disrespect."*

Hamilton: *"I am not conscious of it, sir, but since you thought it necessary to tell me so, we part!"*

And the young man turned and walked away.

Less than an hour later, Washington sent an apology to Hamilton, blaming his outburst on "a moment of passion." Hamilton accepted the apology and came back to work.

But it was clear that the never-ending stress was starting to affect George Washington. And everyone else, too. Joseph Plumb Martin spoke for the entire United States when he said, "I saw no likelihood that the war would ever end."

The Great Race to Yorktown

The year 1781 started out badly for George Washington. In early spring, a British warship sailed up the Potomac River in Virginia and docked at Mount Vernon, Washington's beloved home and plantation. Lund Washington, who was running the plantation while his cousin George was away at war, hurried down to the dock to see what was going on.

Refreshments for the Enemy

When Lund Washington got down to the river, he saw that seventeen slaves had already seized the chance to escape from Mount Vernon by hopping onto the British ship. Then Lund heard the British sailors calling out for service. Bring us food and drink, they demanded, or we'll burn the plantation!

Lund did as he was told.

When Washington heard the news, he didn't seem too upset that the slaves had run away. But he was horribly ashamed that his own farm had provided supplies to the invading enemy. As he told Lund, "That which gives me most concern, is that you should go on board the enemy's vessels, and furnish them with refreshments. It would have been a less painful circumstance to me to have heard, that in consequence of your non-compliance with their request, they had burnt my house, and laid the plantation in ruins."

Another Wasted Year?

And speaking of Washington's troubles, here was his biggest one: it was looking like 1781 was going to be another wasted year—yet another year without a major attack on the British.

At this time, Washington and his army were camped just north of New York City. So was a French army of about 4,000 men, under the command of a general known to his friends as the Count de Rochambeau. Washington had been hoping that this year, finally, the Americans and French would launch a serious attack on the British in New York City. So Washington and Rochambeau spent most of July looking through telescopes, studying the British forts in New York City. They were hoping to find a weak spot to attack. There didn't seem to be a weak spot, though.

Washington was used to disappointments, but this one really got him down. How could he ever win this war? He was having a hard enough time just holding his army together.

And that's when it happened—Washington suddenly saw a way to win the American Revolution. And he could do it right now! He just had to race his army 450 miles south to a place called Yorktown, Virginia.

Why the race to Yorktown? That question really needs a nine-part answer.

Part 1: The King Tries the South

The first thing we have to do is to take a look at things from King George's point of view.

Mighty Great Britain had been fighting these pesky Americans since 1775, and all they had to show for it was control of New York City. The war was costing Britain a fortune—so much that the government had to raise taxes.

King George was feeling the heat. More and more people in Britain were sick of war. They wanted to bring the army home and forget the whole thing. But you know George—he was still absolutely committed to victory over the Americans. So starting in 1779, the king decided to try a new strategy: the British army would destroy the Revolution by capturing the southern states. The famously stubborn King George honestly believed that most people in the South were still loyal to him.

Part 2: Bad Peaches, Bad General

At first, it looked like Britain's "southern strategy" was actually going to work. The British quickly captured big chunks of Georgia and South Carolina.

Then Congress put Horatio Gates (the Saratoga hero) in charge of the American army in the South. Gates showed up in camp in July 1780 and saw that his soldiers were starving and exhausted. So what did he decide to do? He ordered them to march right toward the British!

Hungry enough to eat anything, the men spotted unripe green peaches growing along the road. They feasted—and quickly paid the price. The meal had "painful effects," said Colonel Otho Williams. That was a polite way of putting it. Let's just say the peaches didn't stay in those hungry bellies for very long.

Gates pushed his weakened soldiers on. And on August 16, they ran into the British general Charles Cornwallis and his army at Camden, South Carolina. While Cornwallis was crushing the Americans, General Gates panicked and fled from the battlefield, leaving his entire army behind. He was next seen 180 miles away.

"Was there ever an instance of a general running away, as Gates has done, from his whole army?" wondered Alexander Hamilton, Washington's young assistant.

So far, so good, thought King George.

Part 3: British Behaving Badly

If only the king knew how badly some of his soldiers were behaving in the South.

One morning in 1780 a frightened girl came running up to Eliza Wilkinson's South Carolina home. "O! The King's people are coming!" shouted the girl. "It must be them, for they are all in red!"

Moments later Eliza saw a group of British soldiers riding up to her house. "Where're these women rebels?" they cried, waving swords and pistols.

The soldiers jumped off their horses, ran into the house, and started stealing stuff—jewelry, clothes, pretty much anything that wasn't nailed down. Then one of the soldiers saw the silver buckles on Eliza's shoes. "'I want them buckles' said he, and immediately knelt at my feet to take them out, which, while he was busy about, a brother villain, whose enormous mouth extended from ear to ear, bawled out, 'Shares there! I say, shares!' So they divided my buckles between them."

A few minutes later, it was all over. Eliza watched the British soldiers ride off, their shirts bulging with loot.

This kind of thing was happening a lot. And as you can imagine, the British bandits were not exactly winning new friends for King George in the South. In fact, more and more southern Patriots began rising up against the invaders.

Part 4: The Swamp Fox

That brings us to a South Carolina Patriot named Francis Marion. Marion started leading small bands of militia members on quick, surprise strikes against British soldiers. Marion would march through the night, attack sleepy British soldiers at dawn, then disappear into the forests and swamps, using paths and hiding places the British could never find. "Marion never encamped over two nights in one place," said Tarleton Brown, one of Marion's men.

The British hated Marion, but they couldn't help respecting his creative and daring style. They even gave him a nickname: the Swamp Fox.

Even Continental army soldiers hardly ever got a good look at the Swamp Fox. When Colonel Otho Williams met Marion and his swamp team, he was surprised to see a bunch of hungry-looking men in rags. "Their number did not exceed twenty men and boys," said Williams, "some white, some black, and all mounted [on horses], but most of them miserably equipped."

Miserably equipped, but very effective. With folks like the Swamp Fox around, the British army was never able to gain control of the South.

Part 5: Fight, Lose, Fight Again

General Nathaniel Greene took command of the American army in the South at the end of 1780. And like the Swamp Fox, Greene knew how to use geography to his advantage. His strategy was simple: "We fight, get beat, rise, and fight again."

Doesn't exactly sound like a formula for success, does it?

Actually, it was brilliant. Greene knew his small army wasn't strong enough to actually beat the British. So instead, he decided to lead the enemy on a long and tiring chase all over the vast spaces of North and South Carolina. Once in a while, he'd turn and fight a small battle. And he didn't mind losing these fights, because he knew he was wearing the British down.

Don't get the idea that Greene's army was having a great time, though. Facing the usual Continental army food shortages, the soldiers ate frogs, alligators, or anything else they could catch and cook. And with all the marching and camping, the men wore completely through their clothing by summer's end. "At the battle of Eutaw Springs," said General Greene, "hundreds of my men were naked as they were born."

Well, at least it was warm.

Part 6: Cornwallis Gets Tired

Over in the British camp, Greene's strategy was having its intended effect.

At first, General Charles Cornwallis was determined to catch up to Greene. He ordered his men to toss away all their extra supplies—tents, clothing, even barrels of rum. He hoped this would let his army march faster (and it did, though the soldiers were very angry about the wasted rum).

But Greene always managed to stay a step ahead of Cornwallis. And by the summer of 1781, Cornwallis was frustrated, angry, and exhausted. He reported, "With a third of my army sick and wounded, the remainder without shoes and worn down with fatigue, I thought it was time to look for some place of rest."

So Cornwallis decided to push his army north. Maybe, he hoped, the British would have better luck in Virginia.

Part 7: Spying on Cornwallis

Soon after the British entered Virginia, a twenty-one-year-old named James Armistead decided to help kick them out. But first he had to get permission from his owner—Armistead was held as a slave on a farm near Williamsburg. The owner agreed, and Armistead marched to the American camp.

Armistead met with a young French general, the Marquis de Lafayette (only twenty-three himself). Lafayette explained that what the army really needed was more information about the location and movements of Cornwallis's army. Would Armistead be willing to take a massive risk to get that information?

A few days later, Armistead walked into General Cornwallis's camp and told British soldiers he was an escaped slave looking to earn some cash. The British put him to work. This young guy proved to be very useful to the British. His detailed knowledge of the local geography helped the soldiers find their way around. All the while, James Armistead was sending reports back to Lafayette in the American camp.

Then Armistead took an even bigger risk. He gained the trust of

General Cornwallis and took the job of Cornwallis's personal waiter! This was the perfect position for a spy. Serving food and walking around the dinner table, Armistead was able to see and hear everything that went on in Cornwallis's own tent.

Armistead always had a hard time getting a close look at official maps and plans because Cornwallis was so careful with his papers. As Lafayette explained: "His Lordship Cornwallis is so shy of his papers that my honest friend says he cannot get at them."

Armistead kept working, though, and he kept feeding badly needed information to Lafayette. This helped the Americans keep a close watch on Cornwallis as he marched his army around Virginia.

But exactly where was Cornwallis headed?

Part 8: Pick a Port, Any Port

The truth is, even Cornwallis didn't know. All summer long, he exchanged angry letters with General Henry Clinton, the British commander in New York City. Like most top British generals in this war, these two guys couldn't stand each other. Clinton wanted Cornwallis to come north to New York, because he was sure Washington was about to attack him there. Cornwallis wanted Clinton to come south to Virginia, because he was convinced the British could capture this important state.

They finally agreed on a compromise: Cornwallis would take control of a port town on the Virginia coast. That way, British ships could move soldiers quickly back and forth between New York and Virginia.

So Cornwallis started looking for a good port. He picked a tiny town near the Chesapeake Bay. Welcome to Yorktown, General Cornwallis.

Part 9: The French Sail North

Now there's just one last piece of the Yorktown puzzle. As Cornwallis was settling in at Yorktown, a fleet of French warships started sailing north from the Caribbean Sea. The commander of the fleet, Count de Grasse, thought he might be able to help with the war. His destination: the Chesapeake Bay.

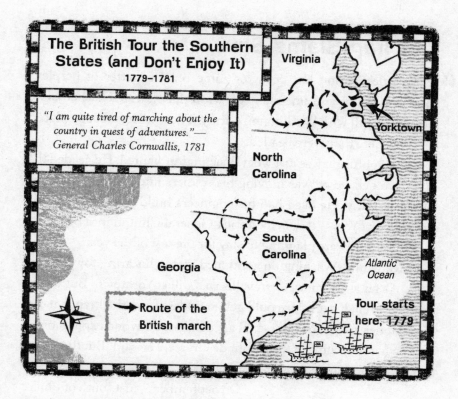

The British Tour the Southern States (and Don't Enjoy It)
1779–1781

"I am quite tired of marching about the country in quest of adventures."—General Charles Cornwallis, 1781

Virginia

Yorktown

North Carolina

South Carolina

Georgia

Atlantic Ocean

Tour starts here, 1779

→ Route of the British march

Now Back to Washington

And at last, we're ready to return to George Washington. Last we saw him, his face was bright with excitement. And this is why: down in Yorktown, Cornwallis and his entire army were in a trap. And the best part was, they didn't know it!

It was just a question of timing. If Washington could quickly march his army south to Virginia, he could surround Yorktown by land. And if the French warships took control of the Chesapeake Bay, they could surround Yorktown by water. Of course, all this had to happen before Cornwallis realized the deadly danger of his position. "We have not a moment to lose," Washington said.

The race was on.

The Trap Slams Shut

"**O**ur destination has been for some time a matter of perplexing doubt and uncertainty," wrote Dr. James Thacher as he marched south with Washington's army. The soldiers actually placed bets on where they were headed.

This confusion was just what Washington wanted. He needed the British to believe he was moving his soldiers into position to attack New York City. He even had his engineers build huge bread ovens around New York—this helped trick General Clinton into believing the Americans were planning to stay for the rest of the year.

Meanwhile, Washington continued racing his army toward Virginia. As far as he knew, Cornwallis was still at Yorktown. But where was that French fleet? He could get no update from the French naval commander, Count de Grasse. "I am distressed beyond expression to know what is become of the Count de Grasse," he said. But there was no way to communicate with ships at sea.

On September 5, just south of Philadelphia, a messenger brought Washington a stack of letters. He opened them and started reading.

At this very moment, General Rochambeau's boat was rowing up to the American camp. Rochambeau looked toward the shore and witnessed a very strange sight:

General Rochambeau

"I caught sight of General Washington, waving his hat at me with . . . gestures of the greatest joy."

As Rochambeau stepped off the boat, Washington ran up to the Frenchman, hugged him, and told him the news: twenty-eight French warships had just arrived in the Chesapeake Bay and were now surrounding Yorktown by water!

Washington rushed his army on to Yorktown and slammed the trap shut on Cornwallis. "We have got him handsomely in a pudding bag," announced the American general George Weedon.

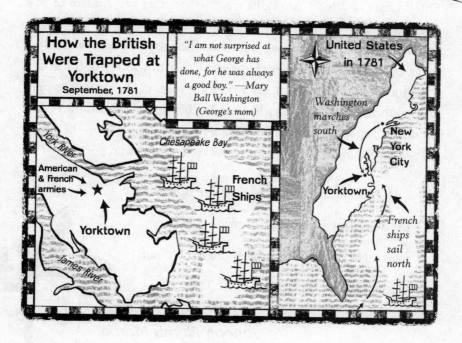

How the British Were Trapped at Yorktown
September, 1781

"I am not surprised at what George has done, for he was always a good boy." —Mary Ball Washington (George's mom)

York River

Chesapeake Bay

American & French armies

French Ships

Yorktown

James River

United States in 1781

Washington marches south

New York City

Yorktown

French ships sail north

Huzzah for the Americans!

More than seven thousand British and German soldiers suddenly found themselves surrounded at Yorktown. Cornwallis begged Clinton to send help immediately. "If you cannot relieve me very soon," he wrote, "you must be prepared to hear the worst." But with French ships controlling the Chesapeake Bay, British ships couldn't get anywhere near Yorktown.

At least Cornwallis still had his trusted waiter, James Armistead. And in this desperate situation, Cornwallis asked Armistead for a re-markable favor—he asked Armistead to go spy on the Americans!

Armistead gladly took the job. He snuck over to the American camp and reported to General Lafayette. Now, as one of the country's first "double agents," Armistead was able to move easily back and forth between British and American camps. He gave Lafayette key intelligence and fed Cornwallis information that was useless or just plain wrong.

Meanwhile, Washington tightened the rope around Cornwallis's neck by inching his soldiers closer and closer to Yorktown. It's fitting that Joseph Plumb Martin, after six long years in the army, was here at Yorktown for the final battle. On October 8, Martin and the rest of the army proudly watched the raising of an American flag, the signal to begin blasting cannonballs into Yorktown. Martin reported:

"About noon the much-wished-for signal went up. I confess I felt a secret pride swell my heart when I saw the 'star spangled banner' waving majestically."

Joseph Plumb Martin

"Huzzah for the Americans!" shouted the French soldiers. Then about a hundred American and French cannons opened fire. The French cannonballs smashed right into buildings in Yorktown. Many of the American cannonballs plopped into the river or landed in empty fields (the French had a lot more practice at this stuff).

The British shot back with everything they had, and the fire-tailed cannonballs crossed each other in the air.

Washington stood out in the open, watching the bombs explode in Yorktown. An officer named David Cobb urged the commander to be more careful:

Cobb: *Sir, you are too much exposed here. Had you not better step a little back?*
Washington: *Colonel Cobb, if you are afraid, you have liberty to step back.*

Washington had worked seven long years for this moment. He wasn't going to miss it for anything.

A Shell! A Shell!

Over the next few weeks, the Americans continued moving closer to Yorktown. The men dug trenches and dirt walls to protect themselves from British cannons. For the American soldiers, the biggest danger came from British shells, or bombs that land in the dirt, sit still for a few seconds, and then explode, sending scraps of metal flying in all directions. As a precaution, Washington ordered his men to yell, "A shell! A shell!" whenever they spotted one of these bombs flying into camp.

This led to a heated debate between General Henry Knox and Alexander Hamilton. Knox thought the order made sense—Washington was looking out for the lives of his men. But Hamilton was eager to prove his manhood. He claimed it was "unsoldier-like" (kind of wimpy, in other words) to cry "Shell!" every time a bomb landed nearby.

As the two men argued back and forth, two shells screamed down from the sky and smacked the ground near their feet. "A shell! A shell!" shouted soldiers. Knox, Hamilton, and everyone else dove for cover.

But Hamilton didn't feel quite safe enough behind the dirt walls. He crawled behind the much-larger Knox (Knox was about six foot three, 280 pounds) and held on to Knox's thick chest for dear life.

After the shells had exploded harmlessly, Knox stood up, straightened out his uniform, looked down at his young friend, and said:

"Now what do you think, Mr. Hamilton, about crying 'shell'? But let me tell you not to make a breastwork* of me again!"

Henry Knox

162   * *protective wall*

The White Handkerchief

Nothing nearly this funny was happening in Cornwallis's camp. "We get terrible provisions now," said one miserable British soldier in Yorktown. "Putrid meat and wormy biscuits that have spoiled on the ships. Many of the men have taken sick here."

In early October, Washington started to see dead horses floating in the York River outside the British camp. The meaning was clear: the British didn't even have enough food left to feed their animals. Sensing that victory was near, the Americans and French kept bombing Yorktown day and night.

Then, on the morning of October 17, a teenage British drummer came out of Yorktown beating his drum. The Americans couldn't hear the drum over the sound of exploding cannonballs, but behind the drummer boy they saw a British officer waving a white handkerchief.

Cornwallis was ready to surrender.

Alexander Hamilton

The World Turned Upside Down

The official surrender took place on the afternoon of October 19, 1781. Altogether, 7,247 British and German soldiers marched out of Yorktown and threw down their guns. They really threw them down—they were trying to break them so the Americans wouldn't be able to use them.

"The British officers in general behaved like boys who had been whipped at school," remembered one New Jersey soldier. "Some bit their lips; some pouted; others cried."

A British marching band played a tune called "The World Turned Upside Down." And upside down is exactly how Charles Cornwallis felt on October 19. In fact, he was so upset by this defeat that he sent a message to Washington saying he was too sick to come to the surrender ceremony.

When Cornwallis finally did meet the Americans a few days later, he was in for one final shock. There in the American camp, proudly wearing his American uniform, was Cornwallis's trusted waiter, James Armistead!

It Is All Over!

Washington wrote a quick note to Congress, telling them the big news. "I have the honor to inform Congress," he began, "that a reduction of the British army under the command of Lord Cornwallis is most happily effected." The news spread quickly, sparking celebrations from Georgia to New Hampshire.

The reaction was quite different in London. When the Yorktown news arrived in late November, it struck Lord Frederick North like a bullet to the chest. Remember, this is the guy who had once so boldly declared, "America must fear you before she can love you." Now he started pacing up and down the room, waving his arms wildly and shouting, "O God! It is all over!"

King George didn't agree. "I have no doubt," he wrote, "that when men are a little recovered from the shock felt by the bad news . . . they will then find the necessity of carrying on the war."

When it became obvious to the king that he was the only person on the planet who felt this way, he got so depressed that he actually tried to give up his crown! He wrote a letter to Parliament, saying:

"His Majesty therefore with much sorrow finds he can be of

no further utility to his native country,

which drives him to the painful

step of quitting it forever."

King George

George's friends talked him out of this rash decision. And the king finally accepted the fact that the United States had won its independence. Peace talks began. Ben Franklin and John Adams, still driving each other crazy, represented the Americans.

One Last Story

The peace talks took two years, and during this time there were a few more small battles in the United States. And it was at this time that one of the American Revolution's most famous soldiers joined the army under the name of Robert Shurtleff. What made Robert famous? Robert's real name was Deborah Sampson.

Sampson grew up as an apprentice on a Massachusetts farm, plowing fields, chopping wood, stacking hay. She was tall and strong and eager for adventure. In the spring of 1782, she tied her hair back, put on men's clothing, and enlisted in the Continental army. She was given a uniform, a musket, ammunition, and a knapsack. No one knew she was a woman.

In a small battle that year, Sampson was cut on the head by a sword, then shot in the thigh. Covered with blood, she was carried to a hospital, where a doctor bandaged her head wound. But Sampson didn't want the doctor to inspect her too carefully—even now she was thinking about keeping her secret. So she grabbed a knife and a bandage and limped out of the hospital.

Out in the woods, she sat on a fallen log and calmly cut the musket ball out of her own leg. "I found that the ball had penetrated my thigh about two inches, and the wound was still moderately bleeding. . . . At the third attempt, I extracted the ball."

She bandaged the wound and hurried back to the army. Soon after, she came down with a terrible fever and was back in the hospital. Too weak to eat, drink, or even move, she lay flat on her bed for days. In fact, other soldiers were pretty sure she was dead. They started arguing over who would get her clothes and boots. She had just enough strength left to signal for the doctor. He bent over to inspect the patient—and this is where Sampson's secret was discovered. But the doctor told no one, and when Sampson recovered she once again returned to the army.

This Is Goodbye

The American Revolution officially ended on September 3, 1783, with the signing of a peace treaty in Paris. Now everyone (even King George) had to admit the United States of America was a free and independent country.

All over the country, American soldiers started heading home. Deborah Sampson took off her army uniform, put on women's clothes, and walked through camp. No one recognized her.

Joseph Plumb Martin, now twenty-three, had dreamed of this day for years. But now that it was here, he wasn't quite sure how to feel. "I can assure the reader that there was as much sorrow as joy," he wrote. "We had lived together as a family of brothers for several years."

George Washington and his officers felt the same mixed emotions when they got together one last time at Fraunces Tavern in New York City. The general lifted his drink in the air and said, "With a heart full of love and gratitude, I now take leave of you. I most devoutly wish that your latter days may be as prosperous and happy as your former ones have been glorious and honorable."

Then he asked each of his companions to come up and shake his hand. Henry Knox, who was nearest, stepped up to Washington and took him by the hand. The room was silent. Every man in the place was trying desperately to keep his emotions under control.

But it was no use—General Knox was the first to crack.

Knox burst into tears and grabbed Washington in a big bear hug. Then all the other officers, tears streaming down their cheeks, lined up to hug their commander.

"Such a scene of sorrow and weeping I had never before witnessed," said Benjamin Tallmadge.

Later that afternoon Washington dried his eyes, left the tavern, walked down the street to the wharf, and stepped onto a waiting boat. He turned and waved his hat to his friends as his boat was rowed away from shore.

Washington stopped by Annapolis, Maryland (where Congress was now meeting), to officially resign as commander of the Continental army. "Having now finished the work assigned me," he told the members of Congress, "I retire from the great theater of action."

Then he traveled home to Virginia to enjoy a peaceful retirement with Martha at Mount Vernon.

That's what he thought, anyway.

What Ever
Happened To . . . ?

 Always her husband's closest friend and advisor, **Abigail Adams** continued offering her political opinions while John Adams served as vice president, and then president of the United States. Some powerful men didn't appreciate Abigail's open participation in politics—but that never stopped her. When she neared death in 1818, John Adams described Abigail this way: "The whole of her life has been filled up doing good."

 John Adams served as American minister to Great Britain after the Revolution, actually meeting his old enemy King George III—it was a short, polite meeting. Following one term as president, Adams ran for re-election in 1800 and was beaten by Thomas Jefferson in America's first truly nasty presidential campaign. Adams retired to his farm in Massachusetts, later calling these years at home with Abigail "the happiest of my life." He died at age ninety, on July 4, 1826.

 After dedicating his entire life to the struggle for American independence, **Samuel Adams** returned to Boston and ran for the House of Representatives in the country's first congressional election. He lost to a thirty-one-year-old. Still not ready to leave politics, and too poor to retire, Adams turned to state government. He was elected governor of Massachusetts at the age of seventy-one. The $2,500 salary was by far the highest he had ever earned.

When American forces prepared to attack the British in Canada in late 1775, **Ethan Allen** was sent ahead to enlist Canadian volunteers. Instead, for some reason, he tried to capture the city of Montreal by himself. Sent to Britain in chains, Allen was later freed in a prisoner-of-war exchange. He settled in his beloved Vermont, where he died in 1789.

After risking his life as a spy during the Revolution, **James Armistead** returned to the plantation of his owner. He remained enslaved until his former commander, Marquis de Lafayette, petitioned the Virginia Assembly to grant his freedom, which it did in 1787. Forty years later, when Lafayette was visiting the United States, the two friends met on the street in Richmond, Virginia. They hugged.

As a brand-new British general, **Benedict Arnold** led several attacks on American towns, even raiding and burning New London, Connecticut, just a few miles from his boyhood home. After the war, Arnold moved restlessly between Canada, the Caribbean, and Britain, dying quietly in London at the age of sixty. "Poor General Arnold has departed this world without notice," reported the *London Post*. Peggy Arnold, with her husband till the end, died three years later, at age forty-four.

"Gentleman Johnny" Burgoyne retired from the British army in 1784, turning instead to his true passions: playwriting and fine London living. He wrote several plays, including the comedy *The Heiress,* which was a smash hit in 1786. He died six years later, at age seventy.

Back in Britain, **Charles Cornwallis** joined the massive public debate about who was to blame for Yorktown. His choice: fellow general Henry Clinton. Cornwallis later went on to serve successfully as military governor of British colonies in India and Ireland. He'd be sorry to see that he is sometimes still referred to as "the man who lost America."

Much to the regret of the women of Paris, **Benjamin Franklin** sailed back to America in 1785. Welcomed home as a hero in Philadelphia, he was soon asked to represent Pennsylvania at the Constitutional Convention. "He is eighty-two years old," said a fellow delegate, "and possesses an activity of mind equal to a youth of twenty-five." After convincing many reluctant leaders to sign the completed Constitution, Franklin still wasn't done—he spent his final years serving as president of the Pennsylvania Society for Promoting the Abolition of Slavery.

Shortly after the Revolution, **King George III,** age fifty, began to suffer from a mysterious illness that doctors now believe to have been porphyria. He experienced intense stomach pain, rashes, confusion, and episodes of what witnesses described as "madness"—for instance, one night at dinner he attempted to smash the Prince of Wales's head against the wall. In spite of the work of ignorant doctors, the king's health improved. He continued to suffer similar attacks until his death in 1820, at age eighty-one.

George Washington's young aide **Alexander Hamilton** went on to become one the main architects of the new American government and economy. Some historians say he was the most brilliant of all the Founders, which is really saying something. But the way he died was not so smart. Caught up in a bitter feud with Vice President Aaron Burr, he agreed to duel Burr with pistols. Hamilton was shot and killed in 1804, at the age of forty-seven.

 John Hancock remained the most popular politician in Massachusetts throughout his entire life, serving nine terms as governor. As he grew older, painful attacks of gout swelled his joints and left him unable to walk. When Massachusetts was debating ratification of the Constitution, however, and it looked like state leaders might vote no, Hancock got involved. He wrapped his aching legs in blankets, had himself carried into the meetinghouse, and announced, "I give my assent to the Constitution." Massachusetts approved the Constitution in a very close vote.

By the way, you'll recall that on the night of Paul Revere's famous ride, young Dorothy Quincy said of her fiancé, John Hancock: "At that time I should have been very glad to have got rid of him." Dorothy and John were married in August 1775. They lived happily together until John's death in 1793.

After serving in the Virginia legislature and as state governor, **Patrick Henry** retired from government in 1791. Heavily in debt, Henry revived his old legal practice—and his reputation as the most exciting courtroom lawyer in the country. One reason he had to keep making money was that he continued fathering children into his sixties. In 1798 his second wife, Dorothea, gave birth to Henry's seventeenth child. Henry died the next year, at age sixty-three.

After serving as the country's first secretary of state, second vice president, and third president, **Thomas Jefferson** began a busy retirement at Monticello, his Virginia home. In addition to designing buildings and founding the University of Virginia, Jefferson made peace with his old political rival John Adams. Jefferson and Adams exchanged more than 150 letters, discussing current events, political philosophy, and the hardships of growing old. Jefferson, like Adams, died on July 4, 1826—exactly fifty years from the day their Declaration of Independence was approved.

Before the Revolution he ran a bookstore, but by the end of the war **Henry Knox** was one of the country's top military experts. Knox served ten years as the first secretary of war before retiring with his wife, Lucy, to a mansion in Maine. Always known as great entertainers, Henry and Lucy immediately won over their new neighbors by inviting more that five hundred of them to a massive Fourth of July festival.

Marie Jean Paul Joseph Roche Yves Gilbert du Motier, also known as the **Marquis de Lafayette,** returned to a hero's welcome in France. He was an early leader of the French Revolution; then, due to events much too complicated to explain here, he fled France and wound up spending six years in an Austrian prison. Thirty years later he made one last tour of the United States. He was greeted like a rock star.

 After leaving the Continental army, **Joseph Plumb Martin** spent a year teaching in New York, then settled in Maine. He married, had a large family, and, at the age of seventy, published a book called *A Narrative of a Revolutionary Soldier: Some of the Adventures, Dangers, and Sufferings of Joseph Plumb Martin.* Martin's book gives us one of the best inside looks at life in the Continental army.

 Thomas Paine continued writing and traveling and offending others with his opinions. After nearly being jailed in Britain, and nearly getting beheaded in France during the French Revolution, Paine died penniless in New York City in 1809. His death went unnoticed, except by a British admirer who secretly dug up Paine's bones and put them on a boat to Britain. No one knows what happened to them.

 Returning to private life after the war, **Paul Revere** ran a hardware store, made bells and cannons, and continued his work as a master silversmith. As always, he was ready to drop everything to protect his town. When it looked like the British were about to attack Boston during the War of 1812, Revere grabbed a shovel and wheelbarrow and helped fortify the city. He was eighty years old.

Deborah Sampson married a man named Benjamin Gannett and had three children. In addition to teaching school, she developed a traveling show in which she appeared on stage dressed as a Continental army soldier and talked about her war experiences. When she died at the age of sixty-seven, Congress awarded her family a special pension "for the relief of the heirs of Deborah Gannett, a soldier of the Revolution."

 George Washington's hopes for a quiet retirement at Mount Vernon were short-lived. First he was sent to represent Virginia at the Constitutional Convention, then he was chosen to be the first president of the United States. "I greatly fear that my countrymen will expect too much from me," he confided in a friend. He served two terms as president—then he was asked to serve a third. He absolutely refused.

George and Martha Washington finally moved back home in 1797, where, two and a half years later, Washington developed a dangerous throat infection. With no idea how to cure this kind of illness, doctors bled him four times and smeared a "medicine" of dried beetles on his neck. Washington could tell it wasn't working. "I feel myself going," he told the doctors. "I thank you for your attentions, but I pray you to take no more trouble about me." Sitting with him as he died, Martha called out, "I shall soon follow him!" Martha died three years later and was buried beside George at Mount Vernon.

Source Notes

When I tell people about what I do for a living, some say it sounds like dream, and some say it sounds like a nightmare. I spend long days in libraries, reading tall stacks of books and taking tons of notes. When I find a story or character I like, I follow leads from one book to another, in search of more details. I sometimes think of myself as a kind of detective—a story detective.

The point is, I ended up reading hundreds of books while writing *King George: What Was His Problem?* Below is a list of the books I found most helpful. If you want to learn more about the people and events of the American Revolution, this list would be a good place to start. I hope it's helpful.

Books About the American Revolution

I started my research by reading a bunch of books about the American Revolution—books that cover the entire war. When you read books like this you don't get too much detail about any one person or event, but you get a great overall picture of what happened and why.

Alden, John R. *A History of the American Revolution.* New York: Da Capo Press, 1969.

Bobrick, Benson. *Angel in the Whirlwind: The Triumph of the American Revolution.* New York: Simon & Schuster, 1997.

Cook, Don. *The Long Fuse: How England Lost the American Colonies.* New York: Atlantic Monthly Press, 1995.

Evans, Elizabeth. *Weathering the Storm: Women of the American Revolution.* New York: Scribner, 1975.

Harvey, Robert. *A Few Bloody Noses: The American War of Independence.* London: John Murray, 2001.

Hibbert, Christopher. *Redcoats and Rebels: The American Revolution Through British Eyes.* London: Grafton, 1990.

Ketchum, Richard, M., ed. *The American Heritage Book of the Revolution*. New York: American Heritage Publishing, 1958.

Leckie, Robert. *George Washington's War: The Saga of the American Revolution*. New York: HarperCollins, 1992.

Lossing, Benson John. *Pictorial Field Book of the American Revolution*. New York: Harper & Brothers, 1859.

Russell, David Lee. *The American Revolution in the Southern Colonies*. Jefferson, N.C.: McFarland & Co., 2000.

Symonds, Craig L. *Battlefield Atlas of the Revolution*. Cartography by William J. Clipson. Annapolis, Md.: Nautical & Aviation Pub. Co., 1986.

Ward, Christopher. *The War of the Revolution*. New York: Macmillan Company, 1952.

Books about the events leading to the American Revolution

After working through the books above, I started looking for sources that describe the causes of the Revolution. I also read a couple of great books about those exciting first few moments of the fight for independence—my favorite was *Lexington and Concord: The Beginning of the War of the American Revolution*.

Galvin, John R. *The Minute Men: The First Fight: Myths and Realities of the American Revolution*. Washington, D.C.: Pergamon-Brassey's International Defense Publisher, 1989.

Langguth, A.J. *Patriots: The Men Who Started the American Revolution*. New York: Touchstone, 1988.

Maier, Pauline. *From Resistance to Revolution: Colonial Radicals and the Development of American Opposition to Britain, 1765–1776*. New York: Knopf, 1972.

Shy, John. *Toward Lexington: The Role of the British Army in the Coming of the American Revolution*. Princeton, N.J.: Princeton University Press, 1965.

Tourtellot, Arthur B. *Lexington and Concord: The Beginning of the War of the American Revolution*. New York: W. W. Norton & Company, 1963.

Books about specific Revolution battles or subjects

As I worked on each chapter, I was always on the lookout for cool stories and quotes from specific events—like Washington's surprise attack at Trenton, or the signing of the Declaration of Independence. Here are some books I read to learn about these events. Since these books focus on just one subject, they give you lots more detail than the more general books listed above.

Bakeless, John Edwin. *Turncoats, Traitors, and Heroes*. Philadelphia: Lippincott, 1959.

Chidsey, Donald Barr. *Victory at Yorktown*. New York: Crown Publishers, 1962.

Dwyer, William M. *The Day Is Ours!: November 1776–January 1777: An Inside View of the Battles of Trenton and Princeton*. New York: Viking Press, 1983.

Evans, Elizabeth. *Weathering the Storm: Women of the American Revolution*. New York: Scribner, 1975.

Ketchum, Richard M. *Decisive Day: The Battle for Bunker Hill*. New York: H. Holt, 1999.

———. *Saratoga: Turning Point of America's Revolutionary War*. New York: H. Holt, 1997.

———. *The Winter Soldiers: The Battles for Trenton and Princeton*. New York: Henry Holt, 1999.

Maier, Pauline. *American Scripture: Making the Declaration of Independence*. New York: Random House, 1998.

Neimeyer, Charles Patrick. *America Goes to War: A Social History of the Continental Army*. New York: New York University Press, 1996.

Schecter, Barnet. *The Battle for New York: The City at the Heart of the American Revolution*. New York: Walker & Co., 2002.

Schoenbrun, David. *Triumph in Paris: The Exploits of Benjamin Franklin*. New York: Harper & Row, 1976.

Vanderbilt, Gertrude Lefferts. *The Social History of Flatbush, and Manners and Customs of the Dutch Settlers in Kings County*. New York: D. Appleton & Co., 1881.

Van Doren, Carl. *Secret History of the American Revolution*. New York: Viking Press, 1941.

Wildes, Harry Emerson. *Valley Forge*. New York: Macmillan Company, 1938.

Wills, Garry. *Inventing America: Jefferson's Declaration of Independence*. Garden City, N.Y.: Doubleday, 1978.

Biographies of major Revolution figures

Every story needs its main characters, right? And one of the best ways to find out about the key players of the American Revolution is to read biographies about them. I often read entire biographies in search of just one or two interesting details to help bring the character to life.

Arnold, Isaac Newton. *The Life of Benedict Arnold: His Patriotism and Treason*. Chicago: Jansen, McClurg & Co., 1880.

Brands, H.W. *The First American: The Life and Times of Benjamin Franklin*. New York: Doubleday, 2000.

Brookhiser, Richard. *Alexander Hamilton: American*. New York: Touchstone, 1999.

Chernow, Ron. *Alexander Hamilton*. New York: Penguin Press, 2004.

Chidsey, Donald Barr. *The World of Samuel Adams*. Nashville: T. Nelson, 1974.

Clark, Ronald William. *Benjamin Franklin: A Biography*. New York: Random House, 1983.

———. *George Washington in the American Revolution*. Boston: Little, Brown, 1968.

Flexner, James Thomas. *The Traitor and the Spy: Benedict Arnold and John Andre*. Syracuse, N.Y.: Syracuse University Press, 1991.

Forbes, Esther. *Paul Revere and the World He Lived In*. Boston: Houghton Mifflin Company, 1942.

Galvin, John R. *Three Men of Boston*. New York: Crowell, 1976.

Holbrook, Stewart. *Ethan Allen*. New York: Macmillan Company, 1940.

Keane, John. *Tom Paine: A Political Life*. London: Bloomsbury, 1995.

Martin, James Kirby. *Benedict Arnold, Revolutionary Hero: An American Warrior Reconsidered*. New York: New York University Press, 1997.

Mayer, Henry. *A Son of Thunder: Patrick Henry and the American Republic*. New York: F. Watts, 1986.

Randall, Willard Sterne. *Benedict Arnold: Patriot and Traitor*. New York: Morrow, 1990.

———. *George Washington: A Life*. New York: Henry Holt & Co., 1997.

———. *Thomas Jefferson: A Life*. New York: H. Holt, 1993.

Unger, Harlow G. *John Hancock: Merchant King and American Patriot*. New York: John Wiley & Sons, 2000.

Collections of quotes, memoirs, and other primary sources by Revolution participants

When you want to find out what life was like during a certain time in history, the best thing to do is to read stories told by the participants in their own words. Here are some books full of stories told by people who played a part in the Revolution—both famous and non-famous folks. My favorites were probably the letters by Abigail and John Adams (they were both hilarious, and not afraid to speak their minds) and Joseph Plumb Martin's book about what it was like to be an American soldier in this war that went on and on.

Adams, Abigail. *The Book of Abigail and John: Selected Letter of the Adams Family, 1762–1784.* Cambridge: Harvard University Press, 1975.

Adams, John. *Diary and Autobiography of John Adams.* Edited by L. H. Butterfield. Cambridge, Mass.: Belknap Press, 1961–1966.

Blecki, Catherine La Courreye, and Karin A. Wulf, eds. *Milcah Martha Moore's Book: A Commonplace Book from Revolutionary America.* University Park, Pa.: Pennsylvania State University Press, 1997.

Commanger, Henry Steele, and Richard B. Morris, eds. *The Spirit of Seventy-Six: The Story of the American Revolution as Told by Participants.* New York: Da Capo Press, 1995.

Martin, Joseph Plumb. *Private Yankee Doodle: Being a Narrative of Some of the Adventures, Dangers, and Sufferings of a Revolutionary Soldier.* Edited by George F. Scheer. Boston: Little, Brown, 1962.

Paine, Tom. *Common Sense and Other Political Writings.* Edited by Nelson F. Adkins. Indianapolis: The Bobbs-Merrill Company, 1953.

Riedesel, Friederike Charlotte Luise. *Letters and Memoirs Relating to the War of American Independence.* Translated from the German by Marvin L. Brown, Jr. Chapel Hill, N.C.: University of North Carolina Press, 1965.

Scheer, George F., and Hugh F. Rankin. *Rebels and Redcoats: The American Revolution Through the Eyes of Those Who Fought and Lived It.* New York: Da Capo Press, 1957.

Thacher, James. *A Military Journal During the American Revolutionary War from 1775 to 1783.* Boston: Richardson & Lord, 1823.

Washington, George. *Washington: Writings.* New York: Library of America, 1997.

Wheeler, Richard, ed. *Voices of 1776: The Story of the American Revolution in the Words of Those Who Were There.* New York: Crowell, 1972.

Quotation Notes

One thing I can't stand about textbooks is that they always have historical characters saying the most boring things. Luckily for us, real people are never that dull. The people who lived during the American Revolution really did say all the daring, clever, foolish, amazing, surprising, funny, and gross things that I quoted in this book. Here's a list of the sources where the quotes can be found.

How to Start a Revolution

"The nation has run itself": Harvey, *Bloody Noses.*
"What greater joy": Langguth, *Patriots.*
"Stand firmly resolved": Blecki and Wulf, *Milcah Martha Moore's Book.*
"If you are men": Harvey, *Bloody Noses.*
"America must fear you" and "I hope we shall": Langguth, *Patriots.*
"Soldier, do you": Langguth, *Patriots.*
"There goes": Zobel, *Boston Massacre.*
"I am clear": Cook, *Long Fuse.*
"There were several attempts ": Langguth, *Patriots.*
"The town of Boston": Commanger and Morris. *Spirit of Seventy-Six.*
"If need be": Langguth, *Patriots.*
"I hope you will": Bobrick, *Angel in the Whirlwind.*
"The distinctions between Virginians": Commanger and Morris, *Spirit of Seventy-Six.*
"The New England colonies": Commanger and Morris, *Spirit of Seventy-Six.*
"If you think": Bobrick, *Angel in the Whirlwind.*

A Sleepless Night Before Revolution

"I was one of ": Commanger and Morris, *Spirit of Seventy-Six.*
"Smith, you will find": Forbes, *Paul Revere.*
"That last I saw": Forbes, *Paul Revere.*
"From these movements": Commanger and Morris, *Spirit of Seventy-Six.*
"As for their king": Langguth, *Patriots.*
"The regulars": Tourtellot, *Lexington and Concord.*

"I told him": Tourtellot, *Lexington and Concord*.
"Come in, Revere ": Tourtellot, *Lexington and Concord*.
"We were halted": Tourtellot, *Lexington and Concord*.
"Sir, may I crave": Commanger and Morris, *Spirit of Seventy-Six*.
"One of them": Commanger and Morris, *Spirit of Seventy-Six*.
"Mr. Hancock was": Langguth, *Patriots*.

Who Fired the Shot Heard Round the World?

"Oh what a glorious morning": Langguth, *Patriots*.
"bring the fine salmon": Tourtellot, *Lexington and Concord*.
"I am satisfied": Commanger and Morris, *Spirit of Seventy-Six*.
"Let the troops": Forbes, *Paul Revere*.
"You villains ": Forbes, *Paul Revere*.
"On our coming": Commanger and Morris, *Spirit of Seventy-Six*.
"This morning": Tourtellot, *Lexington and Concord*.
"If you don't go": Tourtellot, *Lexington and Concord*.
"My husband": Galvin, *Minute Men*.
"Will you let them": Tourtellot, *Lexington and Concord*.
"We were totally": Hibbert, *Redcoats and Rebels*.
"Each sought his own" Tourtellot, *Lexington and Concord*.
"We began to run": Tourtellot, *Lexington and Concord*.
"When I reflect": Commanger and Morris, *Spirit of Seventy-Six*.
"A number of": Commanger and Morris, *Spirit of Seventy-Six*.
"The barbarous murders": Fischer, *Paul Revere's Ride*.
"When once": Commanger and Morris, *Spirit of Seventy-Six*.

George Washington, Meet Your Army

"I was awakened": Commanger and Morris, *Spirit of Seventy-Six*.
"In the name": Lossing, *Pictorial Field Book*.
"I walked with": Adams, *Diary and Autobiography*.
"From your bright eyes": Randall, *George Washington*.
"I am now set down": Washington, *Writings*.
"I this day": Commanger and Morris, *Spirit of Seventy-Six*.
"Ten thousand men": Bobrick, *Angel in the Whirlwind*.
"We worked": Scheer and Rankin, *Rebels and Redcoats*.
"He was so near": Bobrick, *Angel in the Whirlwind*.
"Don't fire": Langguth, *Patriots*.

"They rose up": Commanger and Morris, *Spirit of Seventy-Six*.
"The liberties": Bobrick, *Angel in the Whirlwind*.
"The general does not": Hibbert, *Redcoats and Rebels*.
"Plays were acted": Commanger and Morris, *Spirit of Seventy-Six*.
"These fellows": Scheer and Rankin, *Rebels and Redcoats*.
"I have a particular pleasure": Washington, *Writings*.
"I long to hear": Adams, *Book of Abigail*.

Declare Independence, Already!

"In a little chamber": Adams, *Diary and Autobiography*.
"I believe you are": Adams, *Diary and Autobiography*.
"Here lies the body" Keane, *Tom Paine*.
"The little folks": Adams, *Book of Abigail*.
"And by the way": Adams, *Book of Abigail*.
"Some among us urge": Maier, *American Scripture*.
"The whole time": Adams, *Diary and Autobiography*.
"There must be no pulling": Langguth, *Patriots*.
"When the hanging": Scheer and Rankin, *Rebels and Redcoats*.
"How is it": Hibbert, *Redcoats and Rebels*.
"Would anyone believe": Commanger and Morris, *Spirit of Seventy-Six*.
"The lead": Scheer, *Rebels and Redcoats*.
"The eyes of all": Washington, *Writings*.

Losing and Retreating in '76

"I thought I was": Martin, *Private Yankee Doodle*.
"We expect": Schecter, *Battle for New York*.
"Women and children": Vanderbilt, *History of Flatbush*.
"We were strictly" Martin, *Private Yankee Doodle*.
"It was one of ": Schecter, *Battle for New York*.
"I wish to be": Schecter, *Battle for New York*.
"I only regret": Commanger and Morris, *Spirit of Seventy-Six*.
"We will alter": Martin, *Private Yankee Doodle*.
"The general": Commanger and Morris, *Spirit of Seventy-Six*.
"Great numbers": Washington, *Writings*.
"Ten days more": Bobrick, *Angel in the Whirlwind*.
"My friend Scheffer": Dwyer, *The Day Is Ours*.
"My dear Nancy": Dwyer, *The Day Is Ours*.

"Mother and we": Dwyer, *The Day Is Ours.*
"There were times ": Bobrick, *Angel in the Whirlwind.*
"I had the itch": Dwyer, *The Day is Ours.*
"The floating ice": Commanger and Morris, *Spirit of Seventy-Six.*
"I have never seen": Scheer and Rankin, *Rebels and Redcoats.*
"I determined to push": Washington, *Writings.*
"These, in the twinkling": Dwyer, *The Day Is Ours.*
"This is a glorious ": Dwyer, *The Day Is Ours.*
"A few days ago": Ketchum, *Winter Soldiers.*

Showdown at Saratoga

"be home victorious": Cook, *Long Fuse.*
"He was our fighting general": Arnold, *Life of Benedict Arnold.*
"We have one advantage": Randall, *Benedict Arnold.*
"The carriage": Schoenbrun, *Triumph in Paris.*
"I learnt": Clark, *Benjamin Franklin.*
"I have beat them": Bobrick, *Angel in the Whirlwind.*
"When the weather ": Riedesel, *Letters and Memoirs.*
"When I wrote": Bobrick, *Angel in the Whirlwind.*
"I am very glad": Clark, *Benjamin Franklin.*
"He proposes": Clark, *Benjamin Franklin.*
"Such an explosion": Commanger and Morris, *Spirit of Seventy-Six.*
"Both armies": Ketchum, *Saratoga.*
"Arnold rushed in": Wheeler, *Voices of 1776.*
"I shivered": Riedesel, *Letters and Memoirs.*
"Victory or death!": Randall, *Benedict Arnold.*
"We had been warned": Riedesel, *Letters and Memoirs.*
"Thus ended all our hopes": Commanger and Morris, *Spirit of Seventy-Six.*
"Not one of them": Hibbert, *Redcoats and Rebels.*
"It is true": Schoenbrun, *Triumph in Paris.*
"Assure Congress": Schoenbrun, *Triumph in Paris.*
"Last night": Thacher, *Military Journal.*

Will We Ever Win This War?

"The general opinion": Martin, *Private Yankee Doodle.*
"The army was now": Martin, *Private Yankee Doodle.*
"It was not uncommon": Wheeler, *Voices of 1776.*
"The General": Bobrick, *Angel in the Whirlwind.*

"I am sick": Scheer, *Rebels and Redcoats.*
"We are very comfortable": Wildes, *Valley Forge.*
"I shall never forget": Clark, *Benjamin Franklin.*
"I have several times": Randall, *George Washington.*
"My dear Walker": Scheer and Rankin, *Rebels and Redcoats.*
"A cannon shot": Wheeler, *Voices of 1776.*
"Oh, that I were a dog": Commanger and Morris, *Spirit of Seventy-Six.*
"To tell you the truth": McCullough, *John Adams.*
"John Adams is always": Langguth, *Patriots.*
"I should sooner think": Bobrick, *Angel in the Whirlwind.*
"What ship": Commanger and Morris, *Spirit of Seventy-Six.*
"I have not yet begun": Commanger and Morris, *Spirit of Seventy-Six.*
"This brave man": Commanger and Morris, *Spirit of Seventy-Six.*
"It was awful": Wheeler, *Voices of 1776.*
"Twenty times": Randall, *Benedict Arnold.*
"I am glad": Randall, *Benedict Arnold.*
"You young men ": Lossing, *Pictorial Field Book.*
"Arnold has betrayed me": Randall, *Benedict Arnold.*
"That is not General Washington": Randall, *Benedict Arnold.*
"I answered": Flexner, *George Washington.*
"I saw no likelihood": Martin, *Private Yankee Doodle.*

The Great Race to Yorktown

"That which gives me": Commanger and Morris, *Spirit of Seventy-Six.*
"Was there ever": Chernow, *Alexander Hamilton.*
"O! the King's": Commanger and Morris, *Spirit of Seventy-Six.*
"Marion never encamped": Commanger and Morris, *Spirit of Seventy-Six.*
"Their number": Commanger and Morris, *Spirit of Seventy-Six.*
"We fight": Hibbert, *Redcoats and Rebels.*
"At the battle": Bobrick, *Angel in the Whirlwind.*
"With a third": Commanger and Morris, *Spirit of Seventy-Six.*
"His Lordship Cornwallis": Russell, *American Revolution.*
"We have not a moment " Flexner, *George Washington.*
"I am distressed": Commanger and Morris, *Spirit of Seventy-Six.*
"I caught sight": Chidsey, *Victory at Yorktown.*
"We have got him": Commanger and Morris, *Spirit of Seventy-Six.*
"If you cannot": Hibbert, *Redcoats and Rebels.*
"About noon": Martin, *Private Yankee Doodle.*
"Huzzah": Martin, *Private Yankee Doodle.*

"Sir, you are too much": Commanger and Morris, *Spirit of Seventy-Six*.

"Now what do you think": Scheer and Rankin, *Rebels and Redcoats*.

"We get terrible provisions": Bobrick, *Angel in the Whirlwind*.

"The British officers": Commanger and Morris, *Spirit of Seventy-Six*.

"I have the honor": Washington, *Writings*.

"Oh God!": Commanger and Morris, *Spirit of Seventy-Six*.

"I have no doubt": Bobrick, *Angel in the Whirlwind*.

"His Majesty": Cook, *Long Fuse*.

"I found that": Evans, *Weathering the Storm*.

"I can assure": Martin, *Private Yankee Doodle*.

"With a heart": Scheer and Rankin, *Rebels and Redcoats*.

"Such a scene": Scheer and Rankin, *Rebels and Redcoats*.

"Having now finished": Commanger and Morris, *Spirit of Seventy-Six*.

Whatever happened to...?

"The whole of her life": McCullough, *John Adams*.

"He is eighty-two": Brands, *First American*.

"I give my assent": Unger, *John Hancock*.

"At that time": Langguth, *Patriots*.

"I greatly fear": Randall, *George Washington*.

"I feel": Freeman, *George Washington*.

Index

Go Fish!

GO FISH

STEVE SHEINKIN

What did you want to be when you grew up?

At first, a baseball player, but then I realized baseball players have to be really good at baseball. Writing was always on my mind, too. As a kid, my brother and I would write comedy sketches and draw comics, and I think that got me into the idea of being a writer.

What's your most embarrassing childhood memory?

When my father dropped me off for the first day of first grade, I broke out crying in front of the whole class and said, "I'm not staying!" And then when my father insisted, I said, still weeping, "Fine, I'll stay, but I won't do any work!" Kids in that school never let me forget that scene.

As a young person, who did you look up to most?

Had to be my father, who was a doctor, a pilot, an author, and an all-around cool guy. He just did his thing and didn't seem to care what anyone thought about him, which I found amazing.

What was your favorite thing about school?

I loved hearing stories, and I didn't care much if they were fiction or history or science or what. I always liked writing and illustrating my own versions of stories.

SQUARE FISH

What was your least favorite thing about school?

Spelling and anything to do with grammar. I was just looking back at some old report cards, and a teacher was politely explaining that "language skills don't come as easily to Stephen as to many others."

What were your hobbies as a kid?

As a kid, I loved playing sports with my friends. It didn't matter that we weren't that great; we had fun inventing plays and situations and characters and weaving them into our games. And I loved running around outside and getting dirty.

What was your first job, and what was your "worst" job?

In high school I cut lawns for a few families in our neighborhood. I could get as much as $15 for a few hours of work, which seemed like a fortune. My worst jobs were all restaurant related: busboy, host, bartender. I was fired from two restaurants, both times for not being friendly enough with the customers. I wasn't rude, exactly. I just don't like talking that much.

Where do you write your books?

I have an office at home, but I mostly work at my local library and coffee shops. People tell me they'd love to work at home because then they could sit around in their pajamas. But I don't really like pajamas.

Which part of the process do you prefer, writing or researching? Why?

Researching is way more fun. Like so many writers I talk to, I don't really like writing. I mean, I don't like staring at a blank piece of paper or computer screen and trying to put what's in my mind into words. It takes a lot of discipline and willpower to get started.

What do you do on a rainy day?

Same as most sunny days: I sit somewhere quiet and read and write. At a school visit once, when I described my job, a student said, "So, um, you do homework for a living?" I'd never thought of it like that, and I don't like to, but I guess there's something to it. Except I get to make up my own assignments.

What's your idea of fun?

Doing stuff outdoors, like biking and kayaking. Browsing the nonfiction sections of bookstores and libraries in search of great stories. And eating.

What was your favorite book when you were a kid? Do you have a favorite book now?

Hands down, it was the *Mutiny on the Bounty* trilogy—historical novels about a real-life mutiny on a British ship in the 1700s and the incredible aftermath. These days I'm most into true adventure/survival stories, like Ernest Shackleton's *South*, about being stranded in Antarctica, or Nathaniel Philbrick's *In the Heart of the Sea*, about a whaling ship that was rammed and sunk by a whale, and the terrible ordeal of the survivors.

If you were stranded on a desert island, who would you want for company?

My wife and two kids. I know we'd drive each other crazy, and the kids would fight over coconuts and stuff, but we'd have fun anyway.

If you could travel in time, where would you go and what would you do?

I couldn't pass up the chance to meet Benedict Arnold, George Washington, and all the other big shots of that era. It's so hard to get to know them through history books alone. Then I'd come back to the present and tell everyone what those guys were *really* like.

What's the best advice you have ever received about writing?

First picture what you're trying to say as if it's a movie. Then write what you see as simply and clearly as you can.

 SQUARE FISH

What advice do you wish someone had given you when you were younger?

That you can have many careers, one after the other. The important thing is to pick something and do it all-out. Then, if you want to, try something new.

Do you ever get writer's block? What do you do to get back on track?

Yes, sometimes. Even with nonfiction, you can get stuck trying to figure out how to explain something, or what order to put scenes in. It always helps to step away from the problem and work on something else. But ultimately, sadly, the only solution for me is to work harder.

What do you want readers to remember about your books?

I hope they remember the stories and characters, and I hope they're inspired to find out more about whatever part of the story interests them the most. But mostly I just want my books to be entertaining.

What would you do if you ever stopped writing?

I'd say teaching, but I don't think I'm outgoing enough. I think maybe I'd become a fish farmer. Don't know the first thing about it, but I'm interested.

What should people know about you?

In addition to history books, I also write and draw comics, and I'm working on some ideas for novels, too. Back in my twenties, I made a movie with my brother, a political comedy called *A More Perfect Union*. It showed at a few festivals and got some nice reviews, but then it sort of disappeared. Great learning experience, though.

What do you wish you could do better?

With every book I've ever done, I have moments where I lose confidence and think the whole thing is going to stink. It would be great if this didn't happen every time, but I just can't seem to avoid it.

What do you like best about yourself?
I'm pretty good at not giving up (see above question).

What do you consider to be your greatest accomplishment?
Being a father, which is way harder than being a writer.

What would your readers be most surprised to learn about you?
I don't actually enjoy writing. I love the process of finding stories and hunting down all the little details. It's sort of like detective work. And I love figuring out how to put all the pieces of the story together. But then comes the hard part—writing actual sentences. It's always okay once I get started, but that sometimes takes a while.

Welcome to the Civil War—one of the scariest, saddest, and occasionally wackiest stories in American history!

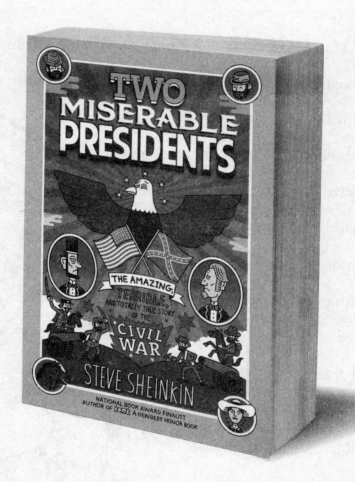

Keep reading for a sneak peek!

How to Rip a Country Apart

On May 22, 1856, a congressman from South Carolina walked into the Senate chamber, looking for trouble. With a cane in his hand, Preston Brooks scanned the nearly empty room and spotted the man he wanted: Senator Charles Sumner of Massachusetts. Sumner was sitting at a desk, writing letters, unaware he had a visitor. He became aware a moment later, when he looked up from his papers just in time to see Preston Brooks's metal-tipped cane rising high above his head.

Stop That Cane!

So Preston Brooks's metal-tipped cane is about to land on a senator's head. Interesting. But before that cane actually crashes onto Charles Sumner's skull, let's step back and take a look at the events leading up to this moment. Because, believe it or not, if you can figure out why Preston Brooks was so eager to attack Charles Sumner, you'll understand the forces that ripped the United States apart and led to the Civil War.

Mr. Brooks, please hold that cane in the air for just a few minutes. We're going to run through a quick thirteen-step guide to tearing a country in two.

Step 1: Plant Cotton

After finishing college in 1792, a young man from Massachusetts named Eli Whitney headed south in search of a teaching job. He wasn't too interested in teaching, though—he really wanted to be an inventor.

Whitney got his big chance when he met Catherine Greene, who owned a plantation in Georgia. Greene told Whitney that plantation owners wanted to grow more cotton. The problem was, cotton had to be cleaned by hand and it took forever to pick the sticky green seeds out of the fluffy white cotton. If only there was a way to clean cotton more quickly, planters could grow and sell much more of it.

Greene set up a workshop for Whitney, and he quickly came up with an invention he called the cotton gin ("gin" was short for engine). Whitney proudly announced the benefits of using his machine: "One man will clean ten times as much cotton as he can in any other way before known and also clean it much better."

Before Whitney's invention, farmers grew cotton only along the Atlantic coast. Now they raced to plant more cotton, forming a wide belt of cotton plantations across the southern United States, from the Atlantic Ocean all the way west to Louisiana and Texas. Plantation owners made huge profits selling their cotton to clothing factories in the northern United States and in Great Britain. Cotton became so valuable to the economy that Southerners declared: "Cotton is King!"

This was great for Southern plantation owners and Northern factory owners. But it was terrible for enslaved African Americans. Planting and picking cotton took huge amounts of work, and that work was done by slaves. So as plantation owners planted more and more cotton, they decided that they needed more and more slaves. The number of people enslaved in the South jumped from just over 1 million in 1820 to about 4 million by 1860.

Step 2: Grow Apart

At the same time, the states of the North gradually ended slavery. This was partly because many Northerners thought slavery was wrong. But let's be honest: it was mainly because slavery just didn't make sense in the Northern economy. Most farmers owned small family farms, so they couldn't afford slaves. And factory owners had no interest in owning their workers—they made more money by hiring workers and paying them a few cents an hour.

Slavery was only one of many differences between the North and South in the first half of the 1800s. Most Americans still lived and worked on farms in both the North and South. But life in the North was changing as more and more people moved to cities and took jobs in factories. Immigrants from Europe were also settling in growing northern cities. Northerners were busy building canals and railroads to connect cities and farms. There was less change in the South, where more than ninety percent of the people lived on farms or in small towns. The Southern economy was based on farm products: sugar, rice, tobacco, and especially "king" cotton.

The North and South were developing different ways of life—so what? These differences mattered because they made it harder for Northerners and Southerners to agree on plans for the future. For example, take the issue of tariffs, or taxes, on imported goods. Sounds pretty boring, right? But tariffs got people excited in those days. Suppose you asked a Northern factory owner and a Southern plantation owner: "Do you support a tariff on manufactured goods imported from Europe?"

"Of course!" the factory owner might say. "Tariffs make imported goods more expensive. So Americans are more likely to buy things made here in our own factories. And that's good for American companies."

"No way!" the plantation owner might say. "We want to buy the goods we need at the best possible prices. Why should we pay higher prices for manufactured goods just to help make Northern factory owners richer?"

Step 3: Keep Your Balance

Now that the North and South are growing apart, let's look at another issue that's about to cause trouble: land. To put the problem simply: What's going to happen with all that land west of the Mississippi River?

As you probably know, the United States started out as thirteen states along the coast of the Atlantic Ocean. But the country had grown quickly:

That Was Fast:
The U.S. in 1776 & 1819

Why is this new land important to our story?

In 1819 there were a total of twenty-two states: eleven "slave states," or states with slavery, and eleven "free states," or states where slavery was illegal. Most members of Congress thought it was a good idea to keep this balance between free and slave states. That way neither North nor South would get too much power in government (or get too angry at the other side).

But everyone knew that western territories would soon be divided up into states—would those new states allow slavery? That was the question Northerners and Southerners were beginning to argue about.

So when Missouri asked to join the Union as a slave state, Congress worked out a deal called the Missouri Compromise. In 1820 Missouri joined the Union as a slave state. And to keep the balance, Maine joined as a free state.

What about all the land west of Missouri? Members of Congress drew a line west from the southern border of Missouri. They agreed that the territory north of the line would someday be divided into free states, and the territory south of the line would be divided into slave states.

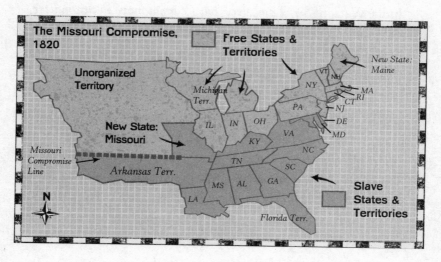

The goal was to protect the balance between North and South. Think it worked?

Step 4: Fight Slavery

Frederick Douglass was not interested in keeping the balance. Born into slavery in Maryland, Douglass grew up working on farms—and thinking nonstop about slavery. How could one person own another? "Why am I a slave?" he wondered. "I will run away. I will not stand it."

When Douglass was eighteen, the man who owned him put him to work in a Baltimore shipyard. One day four white workers attacked him with bricks, knocking him down and kicking him in the face over and over. Fifty white men just stood there watching. Douglass's owner ("Master Hugh," as Frederick called him) went to a judge to complain:

Judge Watson: *Who saw this assault of which you speak?*
Master Hugh: *It was done, sir, in the presence of a shipyard full of hands.*
Judge Watson: *Sir, I am sorry, but I cannot move in this matter, except upon the oath of white witnesses.*
Master Hugh: *But here's the boy; look at his head and face, they show what has been done.*

But Douglass was a slave, a person with no rights. His word meant nothing. The white workers who had seen the beating refused to testify, so the men who had attacked Douglass were never punished.

Douglass continued working (and giving every cent he earned to Master Hugh). And he thought more and more about trying to escape to the North. He knew the danger. If caught, he could be sold to a cotton plantation far to the south.

He came up with a simple, daring plan. In the South, free African Americans had to carry "free papers"—identification papers proving they were not slaves. Douglass borrowed these papers from a free friend who was a sailor. Then he dressed in sailor's clothes, put the borrowed papers in his pocket, and boldly walked onto a train. The train started north through Maryland.

There was only one problem: free papers included a description of the person, and Douglass looked nothing like his friend.

Douglass tried to quiet his pounding heart as the conductor came through the black passengers' car inspecting everyone's papers. "This moment of time was one of the most anxious I ever experienced," he later wrote.

"Had the conductor looked closely at the paper, he could not have failed to discover that it called for a very different looking person from myself, and in that case it would have been his duty to arrest me on the instant, and send me back to Baltimore."

Frederick Douglass

But the conductor only glanced at the papers, then handed them back to Douglass. The train sped north, and that afternoon Douglass reached the free state of Pennsylvania. He continued on to New York. "I found myself in the big city of New York," he remembered, "a free man."

Douglass soon found work in a Massachusetts shipyard. And he became an active abolitionist—part of a movement to end slavery in the United States.

Step 5: Build a Railroad

Frederick Douglass found another way to battle slavery. He used his house as part of the Underground Railroad, a secret system of routes used by people escaping from slavery. Houses like Douglass's were known as "stations"—places where runaway slaves could rest and hide during the day. Daring "conductors," both black and white, guided escaping slaves from station to station all the way to Canada, where slavery was illegal.

The most famous Underground Railroad conductor was a five-foot-tall woman named Harriet Tubman. Tubman grew up enslaved in Maryland, suffering beatings and whippings that left permanent scars on her body. In 1849, when she was twenty-nine, she found out she was about to be sold. She set off on a hundred-mile walk to freedom, helped along by Underground Railroad conductors who guided her to Pennsylvania.

"When I found I had crossed that line, I looked at my hands to see if I was the same person," she said. "I was free, but there was no one to welcome me to the land of freedom." She was thinking of her family—they were all still living in slavery.

"I was free, and they should be free." Tubman said. "I would make a home in the North and bring them there."

Tubman spent the next ten years planning and carrying out at least thirteen rescue missions, guiding about three hundred people to freedom. Can you guess why she liked to operate in winter? The nights were longer in winter, and it was safer to travel in darkness. Safer not only for escaping slaves, but for Tubman too. Angry slave owners were offering a $40,000 reward for her capture.

Only a small minority of Northerners were abolitionists or Underground Railroad conductors. But their work was causing growing anger in the South. Slave owners saw it like this: *Slavery is perfectly legal in the South, and we have invested our money in slaves. Slaves are our legal property. These abolitionists are trying to steal our property. They're trying to make us poor! How would they like it if we came up north and took away their farms and factories?*

You might answer: *But you have no right to own slaves in the first place!* But for now we're not talking about right and wrong. We're just trying to figure out how Northerners and Southerners got angry enough at each other to rip the country in two.

You'll never think of history
the same way again. . . .

Also available from Steve Sheinkin

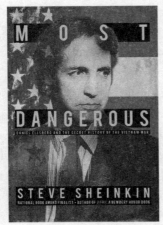

978-1-59643-952-8

978-1-59643-796-8
A National Book Award Finalist

978-1-59643-487-5
A Newbery Honor Book

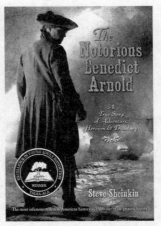

978-1-250-02460-2
A YALSA Excellence in
Nonfiction Award Winner

mackids.com